Animating Liturgy

*The Dynamics of Worship and
the Human Community*

— STEPHEN PLATTEN —

Sacristy
Press

Sacristy Press
PO Box 612, Durham, DH1 9HT

www.sacristy.co.uk

First published in 2017 by Sacristy Press, Durham

Sacristy Limited, registered in England & Wales, number 7565667

British Library Cataloguing-in-Publication Data
A catalogue record for the book is available from the British Library

Paperback ISBN 978-1-910519-54-7
Hardback ISBN 978-1-910519-57-8

In thanksgiving to Almighty God for the Opus Dei

and in dedication to Father George Guiver for many years of friendship and for teaching me so much more about the Opus Dei

and also to Dr Matthew Bullimore for his friendship and for his company in joining in the daily recitation of the Opus Dei

FOREWORD

Rowan Williams

Stephen Platten's essays pose a very basic question to the contemporary Church, which is not likely to be resolved any time soon. The culture we inhabit is one which is uncertain and inarticulate about shared symbolic action; not that it does not have symbolic communal events, rituals of solidarity and celebration, but it does not have much of a vocabulary for speaking about them and making sense of them. And the temptation for the Church is to take this at face value and not to work at making sense of its own shared symbolic inheritance so as to bring out its continuity with what people continue to do in the way of communal symbol-making. When the Church gives way to this temptation, the result is the rather odd situation that prevails in quite a large section of Christian, especially Anglican, practice at the moment: there is a generous and imaginative set of resources for sacramental and symbolic action and for the nurturing of rhythms and structures of prayer; and there is a widespread awkwardness about anything that suggests ritualism and failure in spontaneity or accessibility, indeed a widespread lack of familiarity with these resources. There is something of a gulf between what is (rightly) seen as an immensely positive set of new initiatives in outreach, new styles of Christian belonging and worship, and the world of liturgical revision, canonical patterns of behaviour in worship and so on.

What Stephen Platten does in these brief but very pregnant studies is to invite us to do some thinking from first principles about what is going on in symbolic actions. We are reminded that being human is a matter of organising time and space so that we can better understand our own movement in that same time and space. We narrate and dramatise the process of human change, human growth, human crisis; we use music and theatre to explore our identities, we structure the public and private spaces we live in. We are all of us dismayed and disoriented if we have to spend too much time in spaces that are not meaningfully organised or if we have no way of marking the passage of time (think of how this disorientation has been used as a form of torture). So what we can call in the most general sense a "liturgical" instinct is not an embarrassing religious eccentricity but a routine element in our life as sign-making beings, people who make sense *to*, *of* and *with* one another. What is needed to invite people into the distinctive patterns of Christian liturgical action is not an apologetic minimising of this tradition or an attempt to reduce it to a scheme of teaching aids; rather we need to be ready to walk through both our buildings and our liturgical actions, with confidence and articulacy, alongside those for whom this particular experience is new. We need to be able to show how what we do is precisely a way of organising memory and location so that we both discover a new world that we have in common and are repeatedly enabled to change and develop in that discovery. In theological terms, we must be clearer about how liturgy makes us more fully citizens of the new creation.

It is appropriate, then, that one of the most searching and interesting of these essays deals with "Christian initiation," patiently untangling the knots we have tied ourselves in over "complete" and "incomplete" initiation, sacramental objectivity and personal commitment, and other polarities that lead us down various garden paths. Stephen Platten very reasonably asks: why are these a matter of either-or? It is manifestly true that to be baptised is to become a member of Christ's Body and so to receive the gift of the Spirit so as to be free to address God as Father. Baptism is our entry into the new creation, indeed our *own* new creation. But it has almost always been a matter of more than just some minimal performance. The gift can be both absolutely given and continually learned, and that continuous learning has decisive points of breakthrough and ownership. The mindset that imagines we must approach this in terms of the necessity or otherwise of confirmation as a separate rite ends up giving us a somewhat diminished sense of what initiation itself means. Bishop Stephen's discussion does not offer a final settlement of the question as it has been conventionally put, but it hugely enriches the discussion by sidelining most of those conventional ways of putting it, and focusing our attention on the central meanings of the rites.

Repetition and imitation sound to most of us like unattractive programmes; yet they are foundational in all our human learning, and Bishop Stephen takes us back again and again to the question of what it means to go on re-enacting the shape of the story that has become or is becoming our own. The Eucharist, like the rites of initiation, needs to be rescued from artificial polarities around sacrifice and memorial, and reimagined in a more global way as the showing-forth of a divine action that is absolute gift, self-dispossession, joyful acknowledgement: the fragmenting of our language about it suggests that we have failed to see how the divine action contains more than we can state or embody in any one idiom or any one style of practice. Every Eucharist is one and the same; every Eucharist will bring into focus something that is distinctive. And this may well help us as we try, especially in the Church of England, to find forms or styles of sacramental practice that will work naturally in the world of "Fresh Expressions". To labour the point again: it is important that such new forms of Church life should not be seen as somehow inimical to sacramental and liturgical richness; the challenge is to make the connections with how the meaningful organising of space and time is going on in the lives of people who might not recognise our usual vocabulary.

The Church of England has been very fortunate in having Bishop Stephen's guidance in its liturgical reflections and revisions, and this collection shows why this is so. As he insists, learning the faith in ways that can be effectively communicated means not simply learning formulae or arguments or texts, but learning the "life-skills" of the new creation. And for this we need the gradual accumulation of wisdom about how our space and time are organised for us by the space and time of Jesus' existence. Jesus passes through a narrative of dark and light, action and silence; he traverses the different spaces of the domestic and familiar, the wilderness, the public political world. Traditionally, the movement of the liturgy, especially the Eucharistic liturgy, guides us to follow those movements in time and space, leading us from heaven to earth and from Galilee to Jerusalem and from Jerusalem to the ends of the world, leading us through the cycle of expectation, birth, ministry, death and resurrection. Getting used to living in this environment needs time and space to discover; are we able and willing to provide it in the richness required? That is the challenge this book leaves with us.

PREFACE

As I was preparing this collection of essays for publication, I had first intended the title of the book to be simply *God's Work*, as a translation of the Latin *opus Dei*. On reflection, this title would have been too narrow since the *opus Dei* traditionally has referred to the "liturgy of the hours", or the "divine office". Within this collection is a far wider embracing of the nature of the liturgy and of its setting within the Church and the world. There is, however, good reason for pausing briefly and reflecting on the term "*opus Dei*", since it reminds us that all liturgical worship is an offering back to God for all that we have received through creation and redemption, and notably through the Incarnation in Jesus Christ. Any offering that we make is possible only through God's grace, hence the richness of the term *opus Dei* in reminding us that even our offering in the liturgy is only made possible and efficacious through the power of God's *gracious* gift to us. It is this realization that underpins every act of worship and not only the saying and singing of the divine office, either in community or in the private devotion of clergy and laity more widely. In order to broaden the title and to make it more explicit and accessible, I have instead called this collection *Animating Liturgy*. A deliberate ambiguity is embraced here. The title seeks to describe the part that the liturgy plays most broadly both within theology and in the life of the Church. It also hints, however, at the ability of the liturgy itself to be given life, to be animated. In choosing this title, I attempt to indicate the breadth of topics here embraced.

The opportunity to reflect more deeply on these liturgical themes was made possible most particularly by my being invited to chair the Church of England's Liturgical Commission for a period of almost ten years. Both the work of the Commission itself, and the requests from others outside the Commission, offered the apparatus to study and think further about the Church's liturgy, the fruit of which is represented in these essays. Only one essay came from an earlier period when I had been directly engaged in biblical research, and more specifically on the Gospel according to St Mark. The final essay in the second section is a substantially revised version of that essay, recast for this volume.

Over the years, my experience has offered me the good fortune to reflect and read theology over a wide range of different areas of study. As just noted, this began with a substantial period of research on the New Testament. Later, as a teacher of ethics and moral theology, the focus changed once again, although a background in biblical studies proved to be a useful foundation. Thereafter much of the focus continued to be with students and ordinands leading to more work on ministry, and so ecclesiology. Later still, as head of the small team at Lambeth dealing with foreign relations, that ecclesiological focus broadened with engagement with ecumenical theology, and in particular through my role as Co-Secretary to the Anglican-Roman Catholic International Commission. It is this sense of perpetual motion within theology that gives to this collection something of the variety and breadth that it manifests. Others might describe it, of course, as becoming a theological "jack of all trades and master of none"! Undoubtedly, the entire enterprise has been deepened and enriched by encounter over a period of more than three decades with Brother Harold Palmer at the Hermitage of St Mary and St Cuthbert on the Northumbrian hills north-west of Alnwick. Harold's contribution to the study of the liturgy has been largely hidden. As the recitation of the *opus Dei* has developed there, not only has the worship at the hermitage been strengthened and become more profound, but Harold's learning and experience of performing the liturgy has had a remarkable impact upon others. Father George Guiver's seminal work on the daily office was inspired by Harold and his witness at Shepherd's Law.[1] Through this interaction and its impact upon the late Brother Tristram SSF, so emerged the first edition of the Society of St Francis' *Franciscan Office Book*.[2] Through use in the Anglican cathedral in Portsmouth and thereafter in collaboration between Brother Tristram and Bishop (later) David Stancliffe, further revisions took place which led to the publication of *Celebrating Common Prayer*.[3] This version of the daily office, although inspired by

Anglican liturgical developments, had an ecumenical currency. It was from this book that the final revisions would deliver what is now known as the Church of England's *Common Worship: Daily Prayer*.[4] Although the complete journey has been complex, the origins and inspiration of the current Church of England daily office book lie with Brother Harold Palmer, as indeed does much of the inspiration to engage with the liturgy which stands behind these essays.

The essays fall into three main sections, which are headed successively "Celebrating the Mystery", "Stewarding the Mystery", and "Living the Mystery". The first group are those with a more ecclesiastical stamp. They deal more explicitly with the sacraments, referring both to their history and their celebration; they note too how we celebrate them today. The first essay was the inaugural annual Walter Tapper Lecture founded by the Liturgical Institute based with the Community of the Resurrection at Mirfield. Inspiration for this was an engagement between work with both the Liturgical Commission and the Cathedrals Fabric Commission for England. The essay seeks to relate the givenness of particular church buildings to the liturgy and vice versa. The second essay issues from a challenge to reflect upon the theme of praise within the Eucharist and the significance of this in living the Christian life. The third was a commission to write "as a bishop" on the rites of baptism and confirmation, and the question of what represents a "complete rite of Christian initiation".

In the second section some historical, theological, and practical aspects of the liturgy are the focus of study. The first essay in this section examines three recently published books on different aspects of liturgy. They are written from a Roman Catholic, a Quaker, and finally an academic university provenance and produce an interesting conjunction among them. The second essay started life as a contribution to a Roman Catholic eucharistic congress in Aachen in Germany. It explores a key theme in eucharistic theology. Finally, in this section, comes an essay with an older and longer history originally delivered to a specialist group of liturgical scholars.

The final section of four essays deals with "what theology does". This section has a more theological and ethical bias, and in some ways these essays can be seen to flow out of issues raised in the second section. So the initial piece analyses what it means to live a life rooted in the liturgy.

The second essay, from a symposium to mark the 350th anniversary of the publication of the 1662 *Book of Common Prayer*, examines how the "Prayer Book" has effectively, over that period (and longer if we trace its origins back to 1549), fashioned both community and family life in England, largely through the performance of the occasional offices, but more widely too. In the third essay there is a deliberate attempt to illustrate how the liturgy is itself *missionary* in its impact. Finally, in reflecting on Reinhold Niebuhr, we see that the liturgy can also have a yet wider impact as but one part of what is now generally described as "public theology".

The Church of England's Liturgical Commission was a particularly stimulating laboratory for liturgical thought and this is a unique opportunity to thank all of my colleagues who were members of two commissions from 2005 onwards. Coming from a wide variety of traditions and with varying degrees of professional theological training, these different groups produced enormously fruitful discussion and, of course, published work. Alongside texts to be used in public worship—from a new ordinal to Eucharistic Prayers for use when many children are present—a number of handbooks were also produced during that period. By name I would like to thank those who helped instrumentally in the work of the Commission. These include Canon Peter Moger, the Church of England's first ever Worship Development Officer, and then his successor, the Revd Christopher Woods. The two key link officers with the General Synod were Dr Colin Podmore and Jonathan Neil-Smith, who were crucial in steering legislation through the labyrinthine corridors and paths of ecclesiastical legislation, and to whom we owe an enormous debt. Finally, the redoubtable Sue Moore, who as Administrative Secretary to the Commission found herself caught between every conceivable set of irresistible forces and some immoveable objects. Sue's patience, industry, and, increasingly, knowledge of liturgy and liturgical study became a sine qua non if the Commission was to function at all. Also I would like to register a very warm note of gratitude to the Revd Dr Matthew Bullimore, who read through many of these essays, and often more than once. He is always a constructive editor, critic, and advisor, and he helped greatly in deciding on the best way of putting the essays together with a clear logic for this collection. Most recently I owe an enormous amount to Kay Norman, who has helped bring order out of chaos in these essays, and then finally my thanks to Rosslie, my wife, for her forbearance in putting up with my absence for so many liturgical meetings. My warmest thanks to all, and I hope that they may all enjoy the following essays.

Stephen Platten
Cornhill, London, Epiphany 2017

NOTES

1. George Guiver, *Company of Voices: Daily Prayer and the People of God* (SPCK, 1988; revised edn., Canterbury Press, 2001).
2. *Franciscan Office Book,* Society of St Francis, Hilfield Friary, Dorset (privately published).
3. *Celebrating Common Prayer* (Mowbray, 1992).
4. *Common Worship: Daily Prayer* (Church House Publishing, 2005).

CONTENTS

1.   BUILDING SACRAMENTS[1]

In December 1961, work began on demolishing the great Doric arch or, more correctly, *propylaeum* which had been the trademark of London's Euston Station from the very beginning of the station's existence in 1837; Euston is the earliest of that series of stations built north of Euston Road, the southernmost point allowable by the government for the capital's northern railway termini. The demolition of the arch became a key "line in the sand" with regard to the treatment of London's built heritage. John Betjeman, later Poet Laureate, conducted a vigorous campaign to save the arch but Ernest Marples, the Minister of Transport, and the Prime Minister himself, Harold Macmillan, both refused to allow the arch to be listed and so preserved. Almost two-thirds of the stonework still lies in the bed of the Prescott Channel, a flood relief canal on the River Lee Navigation. It remains the focus of a lively pressure group's efforts to get the arch reconstructed somewhere on the Euston site.

This was an important landmark decision for three reasons. First, it was (and still is) seen as an act of gross Philistinism; second, thereafter both stations and other key public buildings became far less easy to bulldoze, ignoring the environmental lobby: the statue of John Betjeman in the remodelled St Pancras station is an iconic reminder of the poet's part in saving our architectural heritage; third, Euston has come to be used almost as a paradigm of how not to bring architecture and utility into conjunction, or better still, harmony with each other. Visit it at almost any time of the day or night and it remains a monument to inhumane design and planning. The main concourse is a vast featureless box with no artistic or decorative detail to save it. The entrances to the platforms are like entrances to animal traps or rat runs; there is nowhere to sit, no clear pattern for passengers to traverse this great ugly room, and no other human sign of what the space is intended to be.

Happily lessons were learnt, albeit over a complete generation. So Edward Wilson's Liverpool Street, with Charles Barry's Great Eastern Hotel adjoining, was remodelled between 1985 and 1992. It needed sorting out. This time the refurbishment made a significant bow in the direction of the original architecture. It also took clear note of what the station needed to do, making it more rather than less humane. With still greater panache, St Pancras has been re-ordered, using the old dray warehouse below the platforms for reception of Eurostar passengers and reclaiming George Gilbert Scott's great hotel for its original use.

Now it may seem strange to begin an essay on liturgy and church buildings at London rail termini, but there is an essential crossover—to use a railway image. Each of these great buildings—often they became known as "cathedrals of steam"—was erected to say something beyond the purely utilitarian. So Euston, with its fine Doric *propylaeum* and two attendant lodges bespoke the power, influence, and dignity represented in the extraordinary flowering of English architecture in the great eighteenth-century stately homes. Here were the gateway and lodges to that vast estate which was England, with its historic inheritance and its industrial power. Or there is Lewis Cubitt's magnificent King's Cross train shed of 1852, an exercise in supreme simplicity pre-empting most attempts at modernist architecture by almost three-quarters of a century. Here the six low arches at the front of the concourse gave a simple humanity to the vast double roof behind. This building spoke from the start of a confident and clear future and now that statement can once again be appreciated as it was originally intended.

Finally, and pointing architecturally in almost exactly the opposite direction from Cubitt's pre-emptive modernism, we come to its next door neighbour, George Gilbert Scott's neo-Gothic extravaganza—the last gasp of secular Gothic on such a scale. Here stands a quite different miracle. William Henry Barlow designed the widest-arched train shed ever attempted: the base with its dray store of countless cast iron columns was the massive bow-string which held in place the glass arch of this monumental "long bow". More remarkable still is the fact that Scott was quite independently given the contract to design the hotel and other facilities: somehow the two fitted each other perfectly. In his brilliant study of St Pancras, Simon Bradley notes the debt that Scott owed to his own background in church architecture. Architecture and worship were one. Bradley writes of Scott:

> Thousands of waking hours were ... devoted to private prayer, for Scott remained profoundly religious throughout his life, and more concerned with inner states than outward show.[2]

The now sadly redundant All Souls, Haley Hill in Halifax, is perhaps his most splendid achievement. Bradley then picks up the crucial influence of the Cambridge Camden Society in the development of ecclesiastical architecture in Victorian England, notably with the extensive rebirth of Gothic. Bradley reflects:

> The hotel at St Pancras embodies the new directions taken by the Gothic Revival after 1850. The most iconoclastic buildings of that time were designed by other men, notably the monastically austere High Churchman William Butterfield and Scott's former pupil George Edmund Street. But Scott was never far behind, and in the public mind he soon became identified as the leading figure of the Gothic party.[3]

Scott had been influenced by John Ruskin, and notably his *Seven Lamps of Architecture*,[4] although broadly pan-European influences were there too. But here we need not become over-entangled with Scott or Gothic. The point that emerges is broader and deeper. It relates to the extraordinary flowering of architecture during the nineteenth century. In each of the three examples upon which I have focused—Euston, King's Cross, and St Pancras—their architects combined three key elements. First, they were to be beautiful structures in themselves; second, they needed to speak to the people through the way they were to function: so their setting within the landscape and links with other modes of transport—roads and increasingly underground—were essential issues; it was not merely a matter of the internal workings of the building itself. Finally, the buildings pointed beyond themselves.[5] It may seem pressing terms a little far, but they had virtually a secular sacramental significance. They were symbols for something far beyond the simple matter of getting people on trains. Hardwick, Cubitt, Scott, Wilson, and others were *building sacraments*.

———

Curiously, then, we have entered the world of sacramentality from the unlikely departure point of railway architecture. These great buildings embody key principles which apply to liturgy and church buildings. Such principles are not exhaustive, of course, but there are certainly key concepts there—and we have seen how ecclesiastical developments interlinked with the secular. Nineteenth-century England, "the workshop of the world", had not yet allowed the things of God to become divorced from the things of everyday life. One of the most difficult problems that Christianity and the Church *now* face is the mediated nature of human experience. Food, clothing, furniture, and almost all else is bought "off the peg" and with little connection with those who produce it. The sense of relying on the forces of nature and the animate and inanimate elements of God's creation has largely gone. In Victorian times this was not so. The drift from the countryside had just begun. The tasks to which people were now directed in industry were still co-creative with God in shaping human life. Where, then, does this direct us with regard to ecclesiastical buildings and their relationship to the liturgy? Sacraments are notable for taking the ordinary things of life—water, bread, and wine—and allowing them to be transparent mediators of the divine.

A brief reflection on sacramentality itself is illuminating. Holding together a balanced understanding of the mediation of divinity to humanity requires a combination of revealed and natural theology. Barthians may disagree with this assertion, but catholic Christianity has always wanted to hold together an epistemology with roots in revealed theology and natural theology. This in itself has implications for word and sacrament in the liturgy. It implies that sacramentality is an essential constituent of Christian worship and liturgical practice. There is debate between traditions about both the nature of sacraments and their number, but generally not about their part in the tradition. Odo Casel's "mystery theology" roots the sacraments in the history or narrative of salvation.[6]

Sacrament and sacramentality have been stretched or extended beyond simply the seven sacraments, or indeed in more Protestant circles the two dominical sacraments. In a notable sermon Austin Farrer referred to priests (and presumably, by implication, to deacons and bishops) as "Walking Sacraments".[7] More systematically, in his classic analysis of ecclesiology, Avery Dulles (following Edward Schillebeeckx and others) talks of "the Church as sacrament". So he writes:

> ... where the Church as sacrament is present, the grace of Christ will not be absent. That grace, seeking its appropriate form of expression—as grace inevitably does—will impel men to prayer, confession, worship, and other acts whereby the Church externally realizes its essence.[8]

So, for Dulles, the Church is not just a sign, rather it is in its present state generally redolent of God's gracious presence in the world, so:

> ... something of the Church as sign will be present wherever the grace of God is effectively at work.[9]

As a divine-human institution the Church is about people, so Dulles notes:

> Since sacramentality by its very nature calls for active participation, only those who belong to the Church, and actively help to constitute it as a sign, share fully in its reality as a sacrament.[10]

This understanding of the nature of the Church has become an important element in the agreed statements of the Anglican-Roman Catholic International Commission:

> The Holy Spirit uses the Church as the means through which the Word of God is proclaimed afresh, the sacraments are celebrated, and the people of God receive pastoral oversight,

so that the life of the Gospel is manifested in the life of its
members.[11]

This section of the agreed statement on sacramentality begins its final
paragraph noting:

> The sacramental nature of the Church as sign, instrument
> and foretaste of communion is especially manifest in the
> common celebration of the eucharist.

It concludes:

> . . . it is sent out to realize, manifest and extend that
> communion in the world.[12]

One further reflection on sacramentality, this time from a fascinating
biographical account of the poet, George Mackay Brown, his life and work.
Brown was a convert to Roman Catholicism and the priest Jock Dalrymple
reflects on Brown's religious life and beliefs. Noting that the Church is
now often seen as a "secondary sacrament", Dalrymple reflects further:

> The notion of the sacramental is much broader than that,
> though. A friendship can be sacramental, a sunset or a
> rainbow can be sacramental, a view can be sacramental, a
> person saying sorry can be sacramental. George wouldn't
> use that kind of language, but it's about seeing signs of God's
> presence in the ordinary things of everyday life, and not
> just church things.[13]

This may feel like a fairly loose use of theological language, but it certainly
implies a broader use of the sacramental. So if such sacramentality is true
of the Church itself, then what might be said of the buildings in which
the sacramental community meets and in which the sacraments are
celebrated? This question received a fulsome answer from the Cambridge
Camden Society. Two key "Ecclesiologists", Benjamin Webb and John
Mason Neale, translated a thirteenth-century manual of symbolism by

William Durandus, the *Rationale Divinorum Officiorum*. They produced a lengthy introduction to this, setting out clearly their agenda:

> We assert, then, that *Sacramentality* is that characteristic which so strikingly distinguishes ancient ecclesiastical architecture from our own. By this word we mean to convey the idea that, by the outward and visible form, is signified something inward and spiritual . . . This Christian reality, we would call SACRAMENTALITY: investing that symbolical truthfulness, which it has in common with *every* true expression, with a greater force and holiness, both from the greater purity of truth which it embodies . . . [14]

In floreate manner elsewhere in their journal, *The Ecclesiologist*, they wrote:

> A church is not as it should be, till *every* window is filled with stained glass, till every inch is covered with encaustic tiles, till there is a rood screen glowing with the brightest tints and with gold, nay, if we would arrive at perfection, the roof and walls must be painted and frescoed. [15]

Something of that is captured by William Butterfield in both All Saints, Margaret Street in London and in the chapel of Keble College, Oxford. Or, in the Wolds of the East Riding, in a positively dazzling array, with Clayton and Bell wall murals, with floor mosaics and stained glass, George Edmund Street and John Loughborough Pearson created this effect in the amazing church at Garton-on-the-Wolds; fairly recently it was brought back to its pristine splendour through the generosity of the Nikolaus Pevsner Trust. [16]

The Camden Society and its followers saw church architecture as a vocation and not simply a profession. The devoutness of Scott which we encountered earlier was there in so many architects of this era: John Loughborough Pearson commented, "My business is to see what will bring people soonest to their knees." Charles Eamer Kempe, the stained glass artist, had considered ordination. In the twentieth century the tradition continued with Sir Ninian Comper and Stephen Dykes Bower.

The nineteenth-century ecclesiological enthusiasts understandably did not take everyone with them. Nevertheless, if we skim off some of the most exaggerated froth and make proper links with sacramental theology, we can still argue for the sacramentality of church buildings. What was true, in a curious and more secular way, of railway stations is essential to these places built for the worship of Almighty God. They are imbued with a true sacramentality, hence our title here, "Building Sacraments". There is within that title a deliberate allusiveness. Sacramentality, however, is not somehow restricted to the Gothic style. Instead, to talk of building sacraments, or of buildings having a sacramental nature, is to say something about all buildings built for the worship of Almighty God through Jesus Christ. What might this mean in practice?

—

Just a momentary reversion to our discussion of railway termini may help us to address this question. We noted three key issues about the great railway stations of the Victorian age. First, the beauty of the building was an essential starting point. Second, the buildings were designed with a proper sense of purpose and function and with a clear concern for their humanity. Third, the buildings pointed beyond themselves and said something of the society within which they were embedded. If this is true of a secular building it is more profoundly true of a church. Beauty, setting and purpose are all crucial.

Let us begin with the setting. The parish system which has been endemic to western Christendom means that the local church is embedded, but also focal within its own local community. So, for example, Norfolk has more mediaeval church buildings than any other area within western Europe. It is said that at any point one can normally see at least four or five church buildings. Towers and spires across Norfolk help define the landscape and hint at the divine. Mediaeval demography is still made manifest by church buildings, even where villages have disappeared. A similar reflection can be made of our towns and cities where the architecture of the church often makes the building visible from a distance.

Settings vary, however, and this is very clear when comparing cathedrals and parish churches. So St Mary's Cathedral, Edinburgh is set spaciously in the elegant layout of Robert Adam's classical "new town" as if designed to be there, even though it came far later. Salisbury Cathedral sits among the billiard-table-like greens of the Close with its majestic cloister, even though it was never built to be inhabited by monks. Norwich Cathedral and its Close occupy the same footprint given to them by the Benedictine Herbert de Losinga just before the turn of the twelfth century. Truro Cathedral is set hugger-mugger amongst the old houses of that tiny city, packed in to breathe an atmosphere similar to the cathedrals of France. How churches relate to their wider community is essential to the healthy life of these sacramental buildings. Even the positioning of paths and the relationship of paved to grassy areas is crucial to patterns of life in each place. British Home Stores erected a glass-clad building in Wakefield's Kirkgate which reflects almost perfectly the cathedral opposite—so there are in virtual terms two cathedrals. Perhaps that was intended? A similar set of comparisons could be made with the settings of parish churches in villages, towns, and cities. The placing of a church, then, says something of how its founders, architects, and community understood the sacramental significance of the building.

Norwich Cathedral is an instructive case in point. Here in the eleventh century the founder, Herbert de Losinga, a Benedictine monk and one of the new Norman overlords, albeit a priest and bishop, was clear about his task. As with the move of the see from Dorchester to Lincoln and Selsey to Chichester, the Normans set their cathedrals in key centres of trade; here the move was from Thetford to Norwich. Herbert built the cathedral across the main east-west/north-south intersection in this already thriving Saxon city. Still today one can see how these main thoroughfares were diverted by the construction of a great new basilica. Indeed, it is a *basilica* with a cruciform plan.[17] The presbytery is basilican in shape and, uniquely in northern Europe, the bishop's throne is high up in the apse mimicking the role of the Roman prefects. Over the north door he placed an effigy of St Felix. Felix was a second-generation monk from Rome via Canterbury and the key Roman founder of the Church in East Anglia. The pulpitum marks the boundary of the monks' church, the monastic choir. The long nave and the large triforium (or tribune) galleries gave ample scope for processions, with the nave doubling up as the "people's church" and even something of a mediaeval hall for public events. The monastic community, with the bishop as the abbot and the prior running the church, was one chamber of the new beating heart of this Norman city where the castle defined the nature of the other more secular ventricle. The cathedral was a sacramental sign of God's kingdom at the heart of the city and region.

But what of the design of the buildings themselves? Churches, of course, began in private houses, gathering small local communities. This was a common pattern for the first three Christian centuries. Following Constantine's baptizing of the Imperium into the Christian faith, buildings were built "fit for purpose", as we now say, using that rather ugly cliché. The key pattern followed was a secular model. As we see happening later in Norwich, it was basilical and based on the public hall used by the local Roman prefect. The Aula Palatina in Trier survives and for a time was a Christian church. The pattern is rectangular with an eastern apse. The bishop usurps the place of the prefect at the centre of the apse and his chapter or *familia* surround him. Exactly this pattern is still there untouched in the basilica of St Sabina in Rome on the Aventine Hill; even the bishop's chair remains. Herbert de Losinga, in designing his presbytery in Norwich Cathedral, followed this pattern precisely. The Norman overlords made clear their oversight in secular and ecclesiastical affairs alike.

In this past generation this basilical pattern has been rediscovered. Architects Robert Maguire and Keith Murray[18] pioneered this in the new parish church of St Paul, Bow Common in East London and also in the monastic chapel at Malling Abbey in Kent; here the configuration has been slightly marred by the need to intrude four reinforced concrete columns to support the concrete roof which was threatening to fail. Richard Giles' celebrated re-ordering of St Thomas, Huddersfield follows this same pattern, as does his remodelling of the episcopal cathedral in Philadelphia.

Later, different patterns developed. In abbeys and cathedrals where there was the shrine of a saint, the apse might be expanded into a broader rectangular chapel for the shrine.[19] There might even be an ambulatory so that pilgrims could peer over into the "holy of holies" which housed the saint's relics. At Lincoln, on the floor of the east end, successive developments are traced within the expanded space provided by the building of the Angel Choir. Later still, cruciform churches with their familiar transepts began to take over from plain basilicas. In parish churches, the apse often became a squared-off sanctuary concluding a longer chancel. Sometimes the actual architecture of a building speaks sacramentally and theologically. Take Canterbury Cathedral: Henry Yevele's great perpendicular nave is womb-like and speaks of creation. The crossing and "martyrdom" speak of incarnation and redemption. The end of one's eastward pilgrimage in the Trinity Chapel speaks of the Holy Spirit and of the communion of the saints. Hints of the Trinity, then, are also there. Canterbury sits, we believe, on the site of St Augustine of Canterbury's first cathedral, so it speaks too of apostolic history.

The recent re-orderings at Mirfield have also been deliberately designed to make the monastic church of the Community of the Resurrection into a pilgrimage church.[20] The structure of these buildings speaks of the faith expressed in the liturgy. Both Canterbury and Norwich have screens. Screens mean that new vistas will eventually reveal themselves on the journey. At Mirfield, the nave screen has gone but still the Chapel of the Resurrection in the upper church takes one on to a transcendent place. Both Canterbury and Norwich cathedrals are used for pilgrimage and stational liturgies; the buildings themselves are often the focus of pilgrimage by individuals and groups.

Recent liturgical and architectural developments have offered some interesting contrasts. Take four modern cathedrals: Coventry, the Anglican and Roman Catholic cathedrals in Liverpool, and the Roman Catholic cathedral at Clifton in Bristol. Coventry Cathedral, radical and modern in many of its features and artwork, in structure feels like the last of mediaeval buildings. It just predated the impact of the Liturgical Movement. At Liverpool, the Anglican cathedral with its vast central space, whilst being designed fifty years before Coventry, allows for an unexpected flexibility. Its sister cathedral at the other end of Hope Street opted for a circular design with a central altar. Such a pattern, especially with westward eucharistic celebration, emphasizes the sacramental gathering of the Christian community as it celebrates the Eucharist; the family is gathered round the altar. This too, however, has its disadvantages. Some people are still placed behind the altar; also, everyone faces inwards. This neither presents a clear missionary view of the Church looking outwards, or even forwards as with eastward facing celebration, nor is it easy for the outsider to penetrate the circle. The Roman Catholic cathedral at Clifton opted instead for a quadrant floor plan which avoids the problems of a circular design. There are contrasts in new churches too. So in West Yorkshire, the new churches of St Peter, Gildersome and St Catherine, Sandal have followed the Clifton model. In both cases an immersion font is part of the plan. The font at Sandal is over-dominant, but challengingly placed at the entrance of the church; the font at Gildersome is in better proportion to the size of the building, but placed at the side and feels to be more of an afterthought. Both buildings have style and make good use of daylight. The quadrant design speaks well sacramentally, with the community gathering round the altar, but still with a sense of the church building pointing forward, and thus including both a transcendent thrust together with a feeling of being on a missionary journey. It also feels more open to the external world; people can slip in and feel part of the gathered community.

———

Re-ordering also requires the liturgy and the structure of the building to work together to allow the building to echo its full sacramental value. How is the nature and mission of the Church as the Body of Christ expressed through the building and its setting within the community? Put in a more general manner, the question is: how is one best equipped effectively to "build sacraments", that is, to build anew or to re-order a church building so that its sacramental value is both clarified and enhanced? The Cathedrals Fabric Commission for England[21] has sought to answer this question using a model first used in the realm of conservation.

Over the past fifteen years English Heritage[22] and the other environmental and heritage agencies[23] have introduced an element of good practice for all who are responsible for the maintenance and development of heritage buildings. Such individuals and agencies are recommended to produce a "conservation plan". This is a rigorous and expensive exercise since it requires the services of other specialized professions. Nonetheless, despite the energy and expense there is much merit to the process. Church buildings are extraordinary treasuries of our inheritance—almost (one might say) palimpsests where each generation has written over the canvas of others.

But alongside conservation, we should be still more rigorous, focused, and imaginative in relating the liturgy to the development of church buildings. So in pursuit of this, the Cathedrals Fabric Commission now recommends cathedrals also to develop a "liturgical plan". The intention is to produce a clear rationale and understanding of the building. That should seek for an integrity and not approach the building piecemeal. It should include a clear circulation pattern and there should be clarity about how visitors and pilgrims are to circumambulate the building, so that the *mystery* or *narrative* of the gospel is encountered through the sacramental patterning of the building. It should also show an awareness as to how a church building, as sacrament, is expressed in the liturgy. The Roman Catholic rite for the blessing and dedication of the church is instructive here. At one point in the service it notes:

> We now anoint this altar and this building. May God in his power make them holy, visible signs of the mystery of Christ and his Church.

Then later on:

> May it [the church] be a place of salvation and sacrament where your gospel of peace is proclaimed and your holy mysteries celebrated.[24]

If our churches are effectively sacramental of their purpose in being designed for prayer and the proper and imaginative ordering of the liturgy, then all church buildings will be enhanced by preparing a liturgical plan. Such plans will derive from a profound appreciation of the liturgy and of how liturgy and sacrament speak of God in Jesus Christ. That understanding must be integrated with a real understanding of both the architectural history and the later development of the building. In all of this one vital point has been omitted without which all the rest makes no sense. *We* do not build sacraments any more than *we* build the kingdom of God. Sacraments and the kingdom are both of God. Liturgy is, of course, the *opus Dei*. The Community church in Mirfield, and the way it now speaks, that is the product of prayer and a fully committed sacramental life.

NOTES

1. An earlier version of this essay formed the inaugural Walter Tapper Lecture on liturgy and architecture which was delivered at the Monastic Church of the Resurrection in Mirfield on 26 October 2012. First published as "Building Sacraments", in *Theology* Vol. 117 No. 2 (March/April 2014), pp. 83–93, ISSN 0040571X, and reproduced here by kind permission of Sage Publishing (<https://uk.sagepub.com>).

2. Simon Bradley, *St Pancras Station* (Profile Books, 2007), p. 20.

3. Ibid., p. 38.

4. Ibid., pp. 40–41.

5. This is set in a wider context of both landscape and secular architecture in Timothy Gorringe's excellent monograph, *A Theology of the Built Environment: Justice, Empowerment, Redemption* (Cambridge University Press, 2002).

6. See, for example, Odo Casel, *Mysterium des Kommenden* (Verlag Bonifacius-Druckerei, 1952) and also George Guiver, *Pursuing the Mystery: Worship and Daily Life as Presences of God* (SPCK, 1996.)

7. Austin Farrer, *A Celebration of Faith* (Hodder and Stoughton, 1970), pp. 108–111.

8. Avery Dulles SJ, *Models of the Church* (Gill and Macmillan, 1976), p. 65.

9. Ibid., p. 66.

10. Ibid., p. 67.

11. ARCIC II, *Church as Communion* (Church House Publishing/Catholic Truth Society, 1991), p. 17.

12. Ibid., p. 19.

13. Ron Ferguson, *George Mackay Brown: The Wound and the Gift* (St Andrew's Press, 2011), p. 182.

14. William Durandus, trans. John Mason Neale and Benjamin Webb, *The Symbolism of Churches and Church Ornaments, A Translation of the First Book of the* Rationale Divinorum Officiorum (Green, 1843), p.74.

15. Quoted in Mark Chapman, *Anglican Theology* (T&T Clark, 2012), p. 74.

16. Cf. for more detail Nikolaus Pevsner and David Neave, *The Buildings of England: Yorkshire: York and the East Riding* (Yale University Press, second edition, 1995), pp. 433–435.

17. For detail on the Romanesque building at Norwich, see Eric Fernie, *An Architectural History of Norwich Cathedral* (Clarendon Press, 1993).

18. Gerald Adler, *Robert Maguire and Keith Murray (Twentieth Century Architects)* (RIBA Publishing, 2012).

19. Cf. St Albans, Durham, Winchester cathedrals.

20. For background on the development of plans for the original monastic church before the recent re-ordering, see Alan Wilkinson, *The Community of the Resurrection: A Centenary History* (SCM Press, 1992), especially pp. 95–98, 195–200.

21. The Cathedrals Fabric Commission for England is the statutory body which is there to oversee works of conservation and development in the Church of England's cathedral buildings. It was set up in 1990 as a result of the Care of Cathedrals Measure (now CCM 2011) and its work is monitored by the Government.

22. Now known as Historic England.

23. Notably, The Society for the Protection of Ancient Buildings, with the Heritage Lottery Fund also being a key driver.

24. *The Roman Pontifical*: "Dedication of a Church and an Altar", revised 1989 (co-published by Catholic Truth Society in London, Veritas Publications in Dublin, and United States Catholic Conference in Washington DC).

2. IN NEWNESS OF LIFE: EUCHARISTIC LIVING[1]

"*Chairete*," he called in his deep voice, the beautiful Greek greeting, "*chairete, kyrioi* . . . be happy."

The goats poured among the olives, uttering stammering cries to each other, the leader's bell clonking rhythmically. The chaffinches tinkled excitedly. A robin puffed out his chest like a tangerine among the myrtles and gave a trickle of song. The island was drenched with dew, radiant with early morning sun, full of stirring life. Be happy. How could one be anything else in such a season?[2]

Gerald Durrell's *My Family and Other Animals* has been an international perennial favourite since its publication in 1956. Transformed for television, it continues to weave its magic spell. That brief opening quotation suggests why the book touches people's hearts. For alongside the humour and Durrell's perceptive reflections about his family, it is ultimately a celebration of life. The humour itself is part of that celebration, but the focus is broader still. Even, as in that paragraph above, the animal and plant life of Corfu sing the song of happiness. There are countless other extracts in the book which pick up a similar resonant note. Durrell's youthful life on Corfu was formative, indeed seminal. Page by page his book celebrates the beauty of nature and the rich tapestry of human life. The characters, not only from within his own family but all who are caught up into his experience, are drawn with humour and generosity. It is not an overtly religious book, but much of the narrative, and certainly the description of the celebrations in Corfu Town for St Spyridon, the island's patron, capture the same sense of excitement and celebration.

That extract above begins with the Greek word "*chairete*". Durrell translates it as "Be happy." These same words are encountered in the New Testament. In Philippians 4. 4, Paul exhorts his readers in almost precisely the same words: "*Chairete en kyrio*", he writes. Here he means "Rejoice in the Lord" and he refers us to Jesus, the incarnate Lord. Durrell's exhortation, from the lips of Yani, the Greek shepherd, are less portentous. He simply means "Rejoice", or 'Be happy, sir!" "*Kyrios*", in modern Greek, has come to have a less exalted feel; it has become a term of politeness, almost a part of social etiquette. But anyone knowing the New Testament could hardly fail to respond to these echoes of past meanings. Durrell clearly intends a profound sense of happiness and thanksgiving to sound out from the lips of that Corfiot shepherd. It says something about an attitude to life and indeed an attitude to the whole of creation.

Intriguingly, the echoes between modernity and antiquity, between contemporary Mediterranean culture and that of New Testament times, between Yani the shepherd and the life of Jesus, do not end here. For, along with "*Kalimera*" (Good day) and "*Yasas*" (Hello), perhaps the most frequently used word in modern Greece, and so in Corfu, is the word "*Eucharisto*". It simply means "Thanks", and although it is pronounced quite differently from the word Eucharist, it is precisely the same word. So it would not be pressing the meaning too far to say that Greek people (whether they consciously realise it or not) live "a eucharistic life". That same resonant word, which stands at the very heart of the Christian community, is on the lips of Greek men, women, and children morning, noon, and night. It is one of the keynotes of their culture. Who would have thought that one could have found oneself so profoundly caught up into elements of the Christian life starting from a piece of popular literature like *My Family and Other Animals*?

—

Of course, this is only a start. These are but echoes and resonances. It would be unfair to Durrell to turn his magical book, by sleight of hand, into a Christian classic. Nonetheless, it has set us out on the way. For these Greek words take us into the very centre of Christian life down the ages and into the present day. What might this mean for the Christian Church? Both rejoicing and thanksgiving point us to the fundamental Christian description of reality: all is gift.

The title for this chapter is taken from the Church of England's 1662 *Book of Common Prayer*. In the general confession from the Order for Holy Communion, we are called to acknowledge our sins and to repent. Repentance means a radical turning again, and the confession very positively moves on to make us say, "And grant that we may hereafter serve and please thee *in newness of life*, to the honour and glory of thy name; through Jesus Christ our Lord." Newness of life means a pattern of living fashioned after the manner of the Lord and Saviour himself. It is a life rooted in the revolutionary teaching and ministry of Jesus.

The challenge of Jesus' teaching to his own age lay in his radical acceptance of all whom he met and also in his similarly refreshing acceptance of the whole of life as "gift". Again and again Jesus turns upside down the values and attitudes of the world. This is clear in his response to people: sinners and outcasts are welcomed unconditionally; Jesus eats with Zacchaeus the tax collector; he refuses to condemn an adulterous woman: "Those of you who are without sin may cast the first stone."[3] In his healings he often begins with an unconditional forgiveness of sins. Not only does Jesus proclaim these values which describe the kingdom through his responses and actions; they are made clear, too, in his teaching and most obviously in his parables. Luke captures this most vividly in his gospel. The Good Samaritan acts compassionately almost by instinct; the tax collector beats his breast in penitence whereas the Pharisee seems to claim righteousness as his own. The father in the parable of the prodigal son embraces his returning wayward son; he remembers his son as "gift" and receives him back in the same manner. Matthew's account of the labourers in the vineyard indicates that justice and reward are just the beginning. In the kingdom or reign of God, all that we receive is gift and calls out of us our gratitude.

In a Christological analysis, this essence of Jesus' teaching and ministry was captured well by James Mackey in reflecting upon the nature of Christianity and Jesus' witness. The parables, Mackey argues, encapsulate this life of acceptance, giving, and ultimately sacrifice. In these unique

stories Jesus describes what he also lives. Prayer and the Eucharist, Mackey
believes, are the ritual and service which stand at the heart of the way of
Jesus, and the parables offer a pattern of living. So Mackey writes:

> Is there a shorter way of conveying an understanding of this
> experience, at once so complex to the analyst and apparently
> so singular to the one who enjoys it? Probably not . . . but
> if the experience itself could find words to summarize its
> impact in a short space, it would say something like this:
>
> The treasure we can at any moment discover, the banquet
> to which we are all equally invited.
>
> That delay must not mar this discovery, nor decline
> the invitation, for such ingratitude instantly un-graces
> us; it means too that life is more than bread, more than
> accumulated possessions; that to realise the true value of
> someone or something and to discover treasure are one
> and the same imperative act.
>
> That the true value of all that exists is discovered in
> the unique way in which one values a gift; that we should
> therefore not crush by grasping, or tear by trying to pull away.
> The gift has its roots in the giver; like a flower with roots
> hidden that breaks ground to brighten the common day . . . [4]

In these few sentences Mackey captures something of what is meant
in the New Testament by the kingdom or reign of God. It is a way of
living, uniquely revealed in both the life, ministry, and teaching, and in
the passion, death, and resurrection of Jesus Christ. It is a way of living
which is nothing less than participation with Christ and the Holy Spirit in
the life of God. Earlier on, we hinted at something of this from the New
Testament, in Jesus' life, witness, and ministry. It is what Paul describes
elsewhere in the New Testament as "the new creation" (2 Corinthians 5.
16–17). The "reign of God" with the set of responses seen in Jesus thus
has its own patterning power for all humanity in all ages. This takes us
to the heart of the gospel as lived in Jesus. Indeed, it has been claimed
that, "It is this patterning power of the kingdom that gives the Church
its distinctive character."[5]

This pattern, then, is encapsulated in a way of living which receives life and indeed all experience as *gift*. Unexpectedly, perhaps, we find ourselves back almost where we began. Yani, the shepherd, called out, "*Chairete, kyrioi*"—"Be happy, sir!" "*Chairete*" is itself derived from the word "*chara*" which means joy, and this word is closely related to "*charis*" which is the New Testament word which we translate as "grace". The word "*charis*" is rich in resonances; it means graciousness, attractiveness, gracious care, or simply gift. Although he may not have realized it, then, the attitude to life captured in much of Durrell's book exemplifies the essence of the Christian way. In doing so, it helps us to understand still more vividly what this might mean in our own contemporary world. For the Christian this is what life means within the "patterning power of the kingdom". It is the pattern established in Christ, but it is recognizable in Christian lives in every age. Durrell's recapturing of his youthful innocence focuses it perfectly. At root, it is a pattern fashioned by both "*chara*" (joy) and by "*charis*", that is grace or gift. All this triggers within the human spirit the spirit of thanksgiving; of *eucharist*. That spirit can itself transform lives. The rite which above all manifests this is, of course, the Eucharist itself. Let us pause for a moment to reflect further upon the Eucharist, the sacrament of life and of thanksgiving.

—

One of the most vivid pictures of the celebration of the Eucharist springs from Taizé in Burgundy in south-eastern France. The community there witnesses to the life of God's kingdom in its commitment to peace and justice. The Eucharist issues from that same commitment and also nourishes it. The scene there is still more remarkable because of the ecumenical nature of the religious community at Taizé. From across the world, Orthodox and Reformed Christians, Roman Catholics and Anglicans, Lutherans and Mennonites, from all nations and countless ethnic groups, receive communion together. The predominance of young people also enriches the picture that many will have of the nature of Christian community. The action of the Eucharist both makes God's *Church* present through gathering around the altar and also assures all of God's presence there in Jesus Christ.

Fifty years ago, the Anglican Benedictine monk Gregory Dix helped us understand better the nature of the Eucharist. Although understandings of the Eucharist are now more sophisticated, it was Dix who showed the importance of the action and shape of the sacrament. This has helped us see that the Eucharist is not a static rite, but that rather the unfolding drama of the sacrament itself establishes God's *presence* which thus brings us into intimate communion with each other and with God. The proclamation of God's word, the different actions within the "liturgy of the Eucharist" itself, and the sending out all form one integrated whole. At the centre of this stands the great "prayer of thanksgiving".

Thanksgiving is thus not only a synonym for eucharist, it is also there in the solemn central prayer said or sung by the president of the rite. This prayer is variously known as the "prayer of consecration", the "*anaphora*" or the "canon" of the Eucharist. Each of these independently is inadequate as a title for the prayer. "Prayer of consecration" can be confusing, since now the entire sacrament is seen as one integrated piece of "eucharistic time"; time is transfigured as we experience "communion *in sacris*". Thus to look for a specific moment of consecration is misleading. "Canon" too can be misleading; it means, of course, measuring rod or measuring line. It is an identifier of authenticity. Once again it can point too sharply to a specific moment when the bread and wine are believed to be consecrated. "*Anaphora*", a Greek term, comes from the root verb meaning to offer. It has also frequently been used to refer to the whole liturgy and so is richer in its resonances, but even here, the strict emphasis on offering focuses on just one element within a far richer whole. To speak of the great "prayer of thanksgiving", however, weaves all of these strands into its rich tapestry. It reminds us too of the meaning of the entire liturgy, and of the way in which the Eucharist encapsulates a life patterned by the kingdom or reign of God. Eucharistic living transforms lives such that all our experience may then be received as *gift*, as *graced* by God in Jesus Christ.

Throughout its entire length, the great thanksgiving prayer makes all this possible in any number of different ways. So, often the prayer begins with a reminder that we are created primarily to offer God thanksgiving and praise. Then, too, the mighty acts of God in Jesus are proclaimed, in thanksgiving for our redemption: Christ's offering on the cross, his passion, resurrection, and ascension are remembered and acclaimed. There will often also be specific thanksgiving for the saints and a looking forward to the fulfilment of the coming kingdom and reign of God. We pray too, in that great prayer, that God's Holy Spirit will sanctify both us and the gifts of bread and wine; here too is a further focus on thanksgiving. Seminal to the prayer, too, is the act of *remembering* and remembering is indeed a key part of human experience. Plato believed that all learning was remembering. He pictured our lives as being like a journey from a cave out into the world of reality. In the cave there are only images and shadows, copies or silhouettes of reality. As we journey through the cave towards reality, Plato believed that we learn by having our memory of the divine Forms, upon which we gazed before birth, provoked by signs of goodness in beauty in the world. Learning is thus recollection. Christian theology is far more rooted in history and in the mighty acts of God than this somewhat ahistorical narrative. We do remember, but we remember the saving acts of God in Jesus' life, death, and resurrection. As we remember them, so God in Christ is present to us every time we celebrate the Eucharist. In this, we experience the redemption given by God and we give thanks once again for that redemption and for our communion with and in Christ. Hence, every time we celebrate the sacrament, at the heart of the Eucharist, we repeat the words of Jesus, as recorded by Matthew, Mark, Luke, and Paul: we do this in remembrance of Jesus. The host and chalice are elevated to remind us of Christ's sacrifice and to signify his presence to us in the Eucharist. The great prayer of thanksgiving is then a climax within the sacrament of the Eucharist. It focuses the entire life of thanksgiving to which we are called.

—

We have, then, come full circle—back to living eucharistic lives. We have done so, however, seeing how such lives are rooted in the sacrament of the Eucharist itself. This is the place, par excellence, where we are formed by the patterning power of God's kingdom. It is the place where we see, through Christ's own sacrifice, how better to embrace life as gift and to offer ourselves in grace-filled lives. Christ's suffering and death are the culmination of a life of acceptance, of seeing life as gift. The effects of this transformation are seen not purely through the life of the individual. The

Eucharist is itself unavoidably a *corporate* rite. Indeed, another reason why the experience at Taizé is so moving and so vivid is the sheer fact of numbers. Often five thousand or more people, from a great variety of traditions normally separated within different churches, come together to receive communion; the sacrament of thanksgiving sends them out to live eucharistic lives, powered by the mystery of Christ's redemptive sacrifice. This means a transformed community alongside transformed individuals, which has its own theological impact. What might that impact be?

Even within Christianity itself there is a tendency to absolutize earthly principles. This is one of the tendencies which helps keep Christ's Church divided. It also stands at the heart of divisions within individual churches; contemporary problems within both Roman Catholicism and the Anglican Communion stem partly from such absolutizing. This process of absolutizing makes belief in God as a gracious Creator superfluous; the instincts implied earlier on, captured well in Durrell's writing, are sidelined. Life is no longer celebrated or seen as *gift*. Placing thanksgiving at the centre of the Christian's faith is an essential antidote to these tendencies. Thanksgiving is not simply an added luxury alongside other modes and moods of prayer. Instead, thanksgiving for "life as gift" effectively relativizes the claims of earthly absolutes. It also relativizes the claims of dictators and the prophets (profits?) of consumerism and other alternative heavens. Eucharistic living is authentic Christian living. A pattern of living rooted in thanksgiving cannot avoid seeing life as *gift*. In Philippians, Paul puts this in context:

> Rejoice in the Lord always; again I will say, Rejoice. Let your gentleness be known to everyone. The Lord is near. Do not worry about anything, but in everything by prayer and supplication with *thanksgiving* let your requests be made known to God. And the peace of God, which surpasses all understanding, will guard your hearts and your minds in Christ Jesus.[6]

This also places thanksgiving squarely alongside intercession, and reminds us that we *offer* ourselves in prayer rather than simply act as if we are customers in some sort of vast, divine consumer's market. John Pritchard, writing recently on thanksgiving, reminds us, "Prayer is a relationship, not a cashpoint. It's not magic, trying to bend the world to our will. Rather it works the other way round!"[7]

———

We have now seen, then, how thanksgiving is one of the fundamental instincts of the Christian life. We have seen, too, that the Eucharist "incarnates" that principle for us and acts as a focal centre for eucharistic lives. It does so not only in our individual lives but also in its effects upon the Church and potentially in the wider community. How do we see this being made effective in people's lives? One starting point here is balance in both Christian theology and Christian life and prayer. So it is vital for the Christian faith to take seriously the ambiguities of our world and of our experience. For this reason, *theodicy* is an essential part of the Christian tradition. Theodicy seeks to take seriously the problem of evil. How, if we believe in an almighty and loving God, do we explain the existence of evil and suffering? What logic can there be for the occurrence of earthquakes and flooding, of painful and crippling diseases? How, too, do we account for the fallenness of humanity? In his "Essay on Man", Alexander Pope summed this up very sharply:

> Created half to rise, and half to fall;
> Great lord of all things, yet a prey to all;
> Sole judge of truth, in endless error hurl'd;
> The glory, jest, and riddle of the world![8]

All of these questions make it clear that Christian theologians must answer them seriously and responsibly. Indeed, it is that final question about human fallibility that prompts the exclamation within the *Exsultet*, on Easter Eve, "*O felix culpa!*" (O happy fault!). For it was that fault, the hymn reminds us, that helped win us so great a Redeemer in Jesus Christ.

Nonetheless, it is possible for this darkness, this consciousness of ambiguity within our world and experience, to be overplayed. As Gerald Durrell reminded us, there is a very great deal in which we should rejoice and for which we should give thanks. A personal example may suffice. The encouragement of vocations to the ordained ministry and to the religious life is in itself an individual and crucial *vocation*. One such encourager, in our own time, has been a religious who has positively influenced many people over the past two generations. Part of the effectiveness of this ministry of encouragement lies in the ability to point to something of the splendour of our world and of the remarkable opportunities offered in working with people as a minister in God's Church. This individual is a eucharistic person, someone in whom praise and thanksgiving to God for all that we are given is simply instinctive. The instinct of thanksgiving is itself infectious and has nurtured vocations of very varying sorts in a great number of very different people. This is singularly important since there is a sense of self-fulfilment in the way we live our lives. Complaining directs humanity towards negativity. Thanksgiving, praise, and encouragement point in precisely the opposite direction. They fill lives with thanksgiving: they make possible eucharistic living.

Eucharistic living is not limited to the twentieth century. Even a cursory glance through Christian literature down the centuries makes this plain. Nor indeed does the ability to offer thanksgiving depend purely upon the sort of golden experiences recounted by Gerald Durrell from his Corfu childhood. Looking back to the twelfth century, for example, we encounter Peter Abelard, who through his love for Éloise endured untold suffering, indignities, and tribulations. Out of the suffering, however, issued one of the great hymns of praise still regularly printed in our hymn books and sung in our churches. Translated, his hymn "*O quanta qualia*" begins:

> O what their joy and their glory must be,
> those endless Sabbaths the blessed ones see;
> crown for the valiant, to weary ones rest;
> God shall be all, and in all ever blest.

Later in the hymn, Abelard is realistic about our trials and challenges, but still it is praise and thanksgiving that are the instinctive response:

> Now in the meanwhile, with hearts raised on high,
> we for that country must yearn and must sigh;
> seeking Jerusalem, dear native land,
> through our long exile on Babylon's strand.

In the verses of his great anthem of praise, Abelard combines our experience of suffering and of joy, but offers it up in an individual and community song of thanksgiving.

Another very different example of thanksgiving triumphing over grief and tragedy is manifested in the well known diary of Francis Kilvert. Kilvert, an Anglican clergyman in the late nineteenth century, was struck down by ill health and died when he was only thirty-eight years of age. Just two extracts from his diary offer us some of the responses of another very different eucharistic life. First of all, echoes of resurrection:

> An intense feeling and perception of the extraordinary beauty of the place grew upon me in the silence as I passed through the still sunny churchyard and saw the mountains through the trees rising over the school, and looked back at the church and the churchyard through the green arches of the wych elms.[9]

God's creation was often what awakened thanksgiving in Kilvert's heart. Here he captures well the different and contrasting moods suggested by landscape and weather:

> The afternoon had been stormy but it cleared towards sunset. Gradually the heavy rain clouds rolled across the valley to the foot of the opposite mountains and began climbing up their sides wreathing in rolling masses of vapour . . . The Black Mountains were invisible, being wrapped in clouds, and I saw one very white brilliant dazzling cloud where the mountains ought to have been . . . There was not a flake of snow anywhere but on the mountains and they stood up, the great white range rising high into the blue sky, while all the rest of the world at their feet lay ruddy rosy brown. The sudden contrast was tremendous, electrifying. I could have cried with the excitement of the overwhelming spectacle.[10]

Elsewhere in this same piece Kilvert reflects:

> One's first involuntary thought in the presence of these
> magnificent sights is to lift up the heart to God and humbly
> thank Him for having made the earth so beautiful.[11]

This response or reaction is not unusual in Kilvert's writing. It is there
despite the harshnesses of life's experience for him. Such instinctive
thanksgiving does not negate or ignore the reality of suffering. That would
be to allow the theological balance to become equally over-weighted in
the other direction. Suffering, however, which is oblivious of thanksgiving
and eucharist ignores an essential part of Christian prayer.

Another classical example of such eucharistic writing comes again, like
the writings of Kilvert, from a country rectory in Herefordshire in England.
This time the writing springs from the seventeenth century. Thomas
Traherne wrote a series of reflections or "instructions" on the Christian
life which were later called *Centuries of Meditations*, since they had been
composed in discrete collections of one hundred per piece. Traherne,
born in Hereford in 1637, was on two occasions—during the Cromwellian
Commonwealth and after the Restoration of the monarchy— presented
to the living of Credenhill, near Hereford. He wrote the *Centuries* when
he was thirty-five years old, and just two years before his death in 1674.
Traherne himself gave the book no title, but had he done so it would
probably have been "The Way to Felicity". Much of his writing picks up
the theme of felicity or happiness and so captures again our theme of
thanksgiving. He wrote:

> An empty Book is like an Infant's Soul, in which any Thing
> may be written. It is Capable of all Things, but containeth
> Nothing. I have a mind to fill this with Profitable Wonders.[12]

The book was written for Mrs Susanna Hopton in Herefordshire, with
whom he wished to share those "profitable wonders". Just one of his
meditations might frame the broader message he aimed to convey:

> Are not praises the very end for which the world was
> created?[13]

Throughout his *Centuries* this theme remains at the centre. Just two extracts offer something of this mood of prayer and thanksgiving:

> You never Enjoy the World aright, till you see how a Sand exhibiteth the Wisdom and Power of God. And prize in evry thing the Service which they do you, by Manifesting his Glory and Goodness to your Soul . . . Your Enjoyment of the World is never right till evry Morning you awake in Heaven: see your self in your fathers Palace: and look upon the Skies and the Earth and the Air, as Celestial Joys: having such a Reverend Esteem of all, as if you were among the Angels . . . You never Enjoy the World aright, till the Sea it self floweth in your Veins, till you are Clothed with the Heavens, and Crowned with the Stars.[14]

Later in a separate reflection Traherne writes:

> Your Enjoyment is never right, till you esteem evry Soul so great a Treasure as our Saviour doth: and that the Laws of God are sweeter than the Hony and Hony Comb because they command you to love them all in such Perfect Manner. For how are they God's Treasures? Are they not the Riches of his Love?[15]

In all this, then, is embraced the whole of God's economy for the world, and indeed the universe, in the mind, heart, and spirit of Traherne. His reflections offer instruction on how we might begin to pattern our lives after the Kingdom of God. The creation as we experience it at present, our future promised bliss, and also our fellow men and women are brought together within these "profitable wonders".[16] Yet again they describe a world framed by an attitude of thanksgiving. Prayer flows out into a structure and pattern which fashions human life for us both individually and within community.

At this point, prayer as thanksgiving is not far from the prayer of adoration or even contemplation. Prayer at this point is integrally related to the pattern of our moral life. We have seen how such prayer helps us to appreciate "life as gift". It helps us apprehend that element of grace which is at the heart of the gospel. It thus frees us from ourselves. Iris Murdoch, both in her novels and her philosophical writings, applauds contemplative prayer since it helps to unself us. This brief extract from her novel *The Bell* shows what she is about. Dora, one of the key characters, is in the National Gallery:

> Dora was always moved by the pictures. Today she was moved, but in a new way. She marvelled, with a kind of gratitude, that they were all still here, and her heart was filled with love for the pictures, their authority, their marvellous generosity, their splendour. It occurred to her that love at last was something real and something perfect. Who had said that, about perfection and reality being in the same place? Here was something which her consciousness could not wretchedly devour, and by making it part of her fantasy make it worthless.[17]

The answer to her question about perfection and reality is Plato. Plato was foundational for Murdoch, but the point about the pictures and about reality can equally be said of our contemplation, adoration, and thanksgiving to God. God's perfection takes us out of ourselves, God "unselfs us", allows us to embrace life as gift, allows us to live "grace-filled" lives. It changes the basis of our behaviour and of our attitude to the world and of the way we relate to others. This is what Traherne saw in his profitable wonders. More recently, the novelist Salley Vickers has given us a glimpse of this in the unlikely and transformed heroine of her novel *Miss Garnet's Angel*.[18] Miss Garnet's former dry existence where she is turned in on herself is reversed through the experience of the transcendent, and so through thanksgiving. We have increasingly been able to see, then, that thanksgiving as a mode or mood of prayer is positively life-transforming. It lifts us out of ourselves, places us firmly in the hands of God and within the context of the whole of creation and the wider human community. All of this is brought together uniquely in the celebration of the Eucharist. But finally, then, how can this help to understand thanksgiving more widely and outside the confines of the Eucharist itself? Is thanksgiving a mood or mode of prayer which is transferable to *any* aspect or moment within human life?

—

The beginnings of an answer to this question may be discerned in a lyrical section of Paul's second letter to the Corinthians. Paul writes:

> For the Son of God, Jesus Christ, whom we proclaimed among you, Silvanus and Timothy and I, was not "Yes and No", but in him it is always "Yes". For in him every one of God's promises is a "Yes". For this reason it is through him that we say the "Amen" to the glory of God. But it is God who establishes us with you in Christ and has anointed us, by putting his seal on us and giving us his Spirit in our hearts as a first instalment.[19]

Two key points emerge from this brief extract. First of all it confirms our belief that Jesus Christ sets the pattern for the kingdom, that pattern which fashions eucharistic lives, lives of thanksgiving. Jesus offers himself entirely to God: in Jesus every one of God's promises is "Yes". But this leads on to a further corollary: God establishes us and anoints us, giving us his Spirit. God thus stands as the ground of our being, as the reason why life is meaningful rather than meaningless. At the beginning of John's Gospel a similar point is made, but in a very different way. Here God is described as the "Word". Word here, however, translates a Greek word which is rich and multi-layered in its resonances. The Greek word "*logos*" is translated in antiquity in a variety of ways: word, reason, wisdom, purpose, ground—even *meaning*. Picking up Jewish classical resonances, then, God gives meaning to our world and God is perfectly revealed in Jesus who is also the Word or *logos*.[20]

It is in response, then, to the enriched nature of our lives and of our world, as seen in God, that we are provoked into a mood of gratitude and thanksgiving. This is captured perfectly in Paul's image of Jesus, in whom every one of God's promises is a "Yes". Jesus lives out a eucharistic life to perfection and from this the Eucharist itself emerges. So, in one sense, there is no separate mode or mood of prayer which is thanksgiving. It is the context within which all other prayer is formed; it is that context of meaningfulness and gratitude for all—even the trials and sorrows which help fashion our lives. Now we see life as gift. This sets the context for all moods of prayer. *Intercession*, for example, fits into that pattern as we align our wills with the will of God. *Confession* calls us back to a life of thanksgiving when and where we have fallen away from our grace-filled vocation. *Praise* is the natural response to this instinct for gratitude and thanksgiving.

There are, of course, moments in individual lives where thanksgiving pours out abundantly within our prayer. There are countless examples of this—from the birth of a child, to healing from disease; from the exhilaration provoked by God's creation, to deliverance in times of trial. Similarly there are moments for thanksgiving in the lives of communities and nations. Days of Remembrance are also times of thanksgiving. Harvest festivals give thanks for the fruits of the earth. Here are specific moments in the life of our world which call forth from us focused prayers of thanksgiving. In our own life of prayer, too, it is important to remind ourselves of this instinct of thanksgiving. The needs of our world focused in intercession and the penitence expressed in confession for our falling away can both obscure that "ground bass" of gratitude for our creation, preservation, and redemption by God.

One of the new additions to the *Book of Common Prayer* of the Church of England, when it was republished following the restoration of the monarchy in 1662, was the "General Thanksgiving". Written by Edward Reynolds, Bishop of Norwich, it became a classical resource for prayer, usable by people of all traditions. At its heart it captures something of the same spirit that we encounter in Traherne, an all-encompassing response to God for everything that we receive as gift:

> We bless thee for our creation, preservation, and all the
> blessings of this life; but above all for thine inestimable love
> in the redemption of the world by our Lord Jesus Christ,
> for the means of grace, and for the hope of glory.

Later on, rather like Traherne's instructive *Centuries*, it recalls us to live eucharistic lives:

And, we beseech thee, give us that due sense of all thy
mercies, that our hearts may be unfeignedly thankful, and
that we show forth thy praise, not only with our lips, but in
our lives; by giving up ourselves to thy service, and by walking
before thee in holiness and righteousness all our days.

Its position, amongst occasional prayers and thanksgivings in both *The
Book of Common Prayer* and in more recent prayer books, means that it is
obscure for many. It is a magnificent prayer both in its original and in its
contemporary form, that frames all life in the context of thanksgiving. It
makes all life eucharistic, not naïvely ignoring the evils of the world, but
rather allowing thanksgiving to embrace evil as well as good, as a part of
the totality of life's experience. There is another remarkable prayer which
does just this. It was found on a piece of wrapping paper in Ravensbruck,
the largest of the concentration camps for women. It asks:

O Lord, remember not only the men and women of goodwill
but also those of ill will. But do not remember all the
suffering they have inflicted upon us; remember the fruits
we bought, thanks to this suffering: our comradeship,
our loyalty, our humility, the courage, the generosity, the
greatness of heart which has grown out of this; and when
they come to judgement, let all the fruits that we have borne
be their forgiveness.[21]

Thomas Traherne understood the ambiguity of Christian thanksgiving
too, so let him have the last word:

Thou wast slain for me: and shall I leave Thy Body in the
field, O Lord? Shall I go away and be Merry, while the Love
of my Soul and my only Lover is Dead upon the Cross.[22]

NOTES

1. First published as "In Newness of Life: Eucharistic Living", in *The Way*, Vol. 50 No. 3 (July 2011), pp. 7–22, and reproduced here by kind permission of the British Jesuits (<http://www.theway.org.uk>).

2. Gerald Durrell, *My Family and Other Animals* (Puffin Books, 2006), p. 109.

3. John 8. 17.

4. James Mackey, *Jesus the Man and the Myth: A Contemporary Christology* (SCM Press, 1979), p. 159.

5. ARCIC II, *Life in Christ: Morals, Communion and the Church* (SPCK/Catholic Truth Society, 1994), p. 8, paragraph 20.

6. Philippians 4. 4–7 (emphasis added).

7. John Pritchard (unpublished paper).

8. Alexander Pope, *An Essay on Man*, Epistle II, lines 15–18.

9. William Plomer (ed.), *Kilvert's Diary 1870–1879: Selections from the Diary of the Reverend Francis Kilvert,* Abridged Edition (Jonathan Cape, 1944), pp. 133–134.

10. *Kilvert's Diary*, p. 112.

11. Ibid.

12. Thomas Traherne, *Centuries of Meditations*, I. 1.

13. Ibid., III. 82.

14. Ibid., I. 27–29.

15. Ibid., I. 39.

16. Helen Oppenheimer, *Profitable Wonders* (SCM Press, 2003).

17. Iris Murdoch, *The Bell* (Chatto and Windus, 1958), p. 190.

18. Salley Vickers, *Miss Garnet's Angel* (Fourth Estate, 2000).

19. 2 Corinthians 1. 19–22.

20. John 1.

21. See, for example, J. Neville Ward, *Five For Sorrow, Ten for Joy: A Consideration of the Rosary* (Epworth Press, 1971), p. 63.

22. Traherne, *Centuries of Meditations* I. 89.

3.   THE RITES OF CHRISTIAN INITIATION[1]

The publication of the *Common Worship* volume *Festivals* marked the completion of the *Common Worship* project and the provision of authorized liturgical texts for this present generation in the Church of England. There is an understandable resistance within both the Liturgical Commission and the House of Bishops to any revisiting of the liturgy in the near future. Nevertheless, there are still calls to revise further. Nowhere are those calls more frequent than with the rites of Christian initiation. There are perhaps three main causes of tension. First, some believe the present rites to be too unwieldy; there are simply too many words both for regular churchgoers and for the unchurched. Second, there is an increasing feeling that the material can often appear to be marginal to the unchurched culture in which we live. Thirdly, many believe that the relationship of baptism to confirmation has still not been squarely faced and that there are theological and pastoral anomalies because of this. The following reflections focus on these issues and attempt to identify more sharply precisely where these tensions surface.

Let us begin with two different experiences. Both are actual cases in point and the contrast is between the content and pattern of the rite in each case. The first case suggests quite sharply a "lack of fit" between pastoral response and theological/ecclesiological intentions.[2] This first example is set in an aspiring residential suburb on the north-west edge of a Northern town. The church door and main pathway face directly (and tellingly) towards the local hospice which cares for the terminally ill. The task of the Church of God in preparing us all for our mortality could not be more clearly focused. In the season of the resurrection, there is a parish Eucharist. Half an hour after the conclusion of the Eucharist there is then a service of Holy Baptism. There are three candidates—all infants. The total congregation numbers about fifty, only two of whom are part of the regular worshipping congregation. The rite begins with the introductory words which conclude:

> People of God, will you welcome these children
> and uphold them in their new life in Christ?

This is followed immediately by the questions to the godparents:

> Will you pray for them [the children],
> draw them by your example into the community of faith
> and walk with them in the way of Christ?
>
> In baptism these children begin their journey in faith.
> You speak for them today.
> Will you care for them,
> and help them to take their place
> within the life and worship of Christ's Church?

Then follow the questions and answers of "The Decision", reaching their sharpest point with the exchange:

> Do you submit to Christ as Lord?
> *I submit to Christ.*[3]

In the context of a church one-third full—much emptier than at the immediately preceding Eucharist—the full irony of these questions may reveal themselves to us. How can we frame them within this rite to make sense of what we were doing and to avoid arrant hypocrisy? After all, there are virtually none of the regular worshippers present. It gets no easier as the rite proceeds. Towards the end of the service we reflect:

> . . . As they grow up, they will need the help and
> encouragement of the Christian community . . . As part

of the Church of Christ, we all have a duty to support them
by prayer, example and teaching.

Where is this Christian "community", and how does this rite (of specifically
Christian initiation) make sense in this context? Perhaps we might even
ask if the rite is too *ambitious* in what it aims to encompass?

In his helpful review of David Thompson's *Baptism, Church and Society
in Modern Britain*, Jeremy Morris quotes Thompson on just this dilemma:

> How far has the wish to recover some of the significance
> attached to baptism in the patristic period, with its greater
> sense of the Church as a separated society, necessarily
> made it more difficult for the Church to seem to welcome
> everyone who comes?[4]

Morris points out that Thompson's argument shows how a "two-pronged
movement both affirming sacramentalism and the significance of personal
faith (briefly, a movement in part facilitated but not ultimately effected by
declaratory views of baptism) if anything reinforced, rather than undercut,
this growing gap between Church and society."[5]

This very point is, perhaps, emphasized by the Liturgical Commission's
own commentary on the *Common Worship* baptism rite. Within the
section headed "A theological framework", the commentary notes as its
first point that baptism involves:

> *separation* from this world—that is, the world alienated from
> God, and [secondly] *reception* into a universal community
> centred on God . . . [6]

One can hardly fault the theological argument which continues by stressing
how children can grow into the fullness of the pattern of Christ's life
within a community whose mission it is to serve, in the power of God's
Spirit, in Christ's action of redeeming the world. Undoubtedly this was
the vision (if not explicitly stated) of that suburban parish. An "open"
baptism policy is intended, but the impact of the words of the liturgy is

to emphasize the gulf between communities instead of offering a model where there is a clear and safe bridge across that gulf.[7]

The gulf will not always seem quite as stark. The second case is a baptism and confirmation at a college chapel in one of the ancient universities. In the context of Haydn's *Missa Brevis*, with anthems by Jonathan Dove and Morten Lauridsen along with a substantial choir and congregation, it all feels very different, as indeed it may in a cathedral baptism and confirmation service set up as a "staged rite". Here the two communities coalesce to a degree. Here, too, the sense of the Christian life as a journey is much clearer. Initiation is no longer an abrupt confrontation between two apparently segregated communities.

—

In the first of the two volumes that make up *A Companion to Common Worship*, edited by the liturgist Paul Bradshaw, a brief history of the development of the rites of Christian initiation is set out, starting in New Testament times. Later in this historical summary is included material on the Reformation and then the development of these rites in the Church of England in the twentieth century.

Let us begin with the Reformation, when the rite of confirmation underwent some of its most radical changes. The conservative 1549 *Book of Common Prayer* not only retained a rite of confirmation but re-affirmed the English mediaeval rule that "there shall none be admitted to the Holy Communion, until such time as he be confirmed." The 1552 revisions were more radical and the rubrics suggest that the term "confirm" was now being used, at least partially, in a different sense. Instead of the bishop confirming the candidate by the laying on of hands, invoking the Holy Spirit, a stronger sense is offered of the candidate confirming his or her faith in the promises made by godparents at the time of baptism. The shift in the prayers is telling. The 1549 prayer runs thus:

> . . . send down from heaven we beseech thee, (O Lord)
> upon them thy holy Ghost the comforter . . .

In the 1552 rite we read:

> ... strengthen them, we beseech thee, (O Lord) with the
> holy ghost the comforter ...

There is still, as we can see, an invocation of the Holy Spirit to strengthen the candidate but, as we note later, the precise intention of these changes can be variously interpreted. In the rite of 1549, confirmation still appears to be a rite of chrismation with a sacramentally effective invocation of the Spirit. In the rite of 1552, however, the Spirit emphasizes strengthening from within.[8] These are small changes but, under the influence of Martin Bucer, they are suggestive of wider religious, societal, and ideological changes. Indeed, a greater emphasis on interiority in 1552 bears witness to a world becoming less at ease with sacramentalism and increasingly concerned with "personal" belief. In the 1662 *Book of Common Prayer*, both the baptism and confirmation rites remained substantially unchanged from those accepted in the Elizabethan settlement, in the 1559 Prayer Book. Confirmation remained a ratification and so, literally, a confirmation of baptismal promises. While not being "necessary for salvation" confirmation remained integral to the rites of initiation. The rubric relating to communion was softened to read, "And there shall none be admitted to the holy Communion, until such time as he be confirmed, or be ready and desirous to be confirmed."

The proposed revision of 1927/8 effectively intended to strengthen the integrity of the rites of initiation including confirmation. Bradshaw's *Companion* notes, "Confirmation underwent a more substantial theological shift: the preface claimed that, following the example of the Apostles in Acts 8, 'a special gift of the Holy Spirit is bestowed through the laying on of hands with prayer.'"[9] This shift re-asserts the emphasis stressed in the pneumatology of the 1549 Prayer Book. The renewal of baptismal vows was extended and included a renunciation, an affirmation of faith, and a promise of lifelong obedience. It was the period after this that saw both the publication of a series of reports and the beginning of an intense debate on the relationship between baptism and confirmation. Leading the battle groups on behalf of confirmation was Gregory Dix, who saw confirmation (as implied in 1928) as the completion of initiation by the conferring of the gift of the Spirit. Geoffrey Lampe led the opposing brigades, arguing that the fullness of Christian initiation was there in baptism alone. The

1971 Report of the Ely Commission, chaired by Edward Roberts, the then Bishop of Ely, with Geoffrey Lampe as a key member, continued the pressure to see baptism as complete sacramental initiation.[10] The 1980 *Alternative Service Book* attempted to address this controversy by opting for a complete Christian initiation expressed in a unitary rite of Baptism, Confirmation, and Eucharist.[11] If anything, the theology of confirmation became thinner still, although the need for confirmation as a rite for adults returning to faith, or discovering a new and active faith, became more significant. The need for some form of post-baptismal rite thus increased although its theological foundations were not secured.

Paul Avis, in a number of different essays, has taken up the argument as it has been rehearsed more recently.[12] In these articles, Avis has indicated why the notion of baptism being complete sacramental initiation has gained such wide credence. The reasons he notes are the crucial significance of baptism, the need to regain a unified rite, and the essential role baptism plays in the scheme of salvation. Avis argues, however, that this approach to initiation has clear fault-lines. First of all, even if we are unhappy with describing initiation as a *process*, nevertheless it is still appropriate to see initiation as an "unfolding event", a play set in a series of acts. Secondly, within our sacramental understanding of baptism there is the need for human response. Just as the Christian gospel implies the priority of grace, to which we as human persons respond, so baptism is one of the effective identifiers of this. Human response itself unfolds over a period of time; we wrote earlier of the journey or pilgrimage elements within Christian experience. Finally, Avis makes it clear how, in ecumenical dialogue, most notably with Baptist churches, this broader view of initiation offers its own richness. Both infant baptism as practised by some churches and adult baptism, as required in the Baptist tradition, can be seen as part of an extended process which varies within traditions.

Avis notes at one point, "However, it is significant that *Common Worship* has not embraced BACSI [baptism as 'complete sacramental initiation']. In this respect, it continues the tradition of the Book of Common Prayer."[13] This effectively adverts to a continuing debate for, by contrast, the *Companion to Common Worship* notes, "The change of emphasis which now sees baptism as complete initiation has led to baptism with confirmation being a second section of the initiation services."[14] The point is made that chrism may now be used in the baptism rite and that this effectively undermines arguments which see confirmation as the completion of the initiation rite.[15] Later we read:

> Behind all this lies a lack of clear theology of the place of confirmation. The Church of England seems to hold on to it as a necessity, but with little theological justification. One hundred and fifty years of debate have still not led to a conclusion, and the debate seems set to continue. How long will it be before the Church of England is bold enough to include confirmation as a "pastoral rite", as did the Episcopal Church of the USA in 1979?[16]

There is certainly truth in the claim that there has been a lack of clarity about how the Church of England has viewed confirmation. This does not, however, imply that the conclusion arrived at in the *Companion* is itself a necessary one either. Indeed, it is not argued out theologically here. Avis, too, discerns a degree of theological uncertainty which calls for further debate. He notes:

> Obviously, this discussion leaves several questions unanswered. It does not clarify what the nature of the blessing or gift of the Holy Spirit imparted at confirmation is.[17]

Having asserted that baptism is not complete sacramental initiation, and that confession of one's own faith, a laying on of hands at confirmation as a sacramental action, and first communion are part of one unfolding event, Avis argues that now:

> . . . we may be in a more favourable position to begin to fill out the theological and pastoral reconstruction of Christian initiation.[18]

This discussion, then, moves us further in the direction of reflection upon the theology of confirmation. At this point it may help to take stock. Where precisely does the argument lie in relation to confirmation as part of an unfolding event? There is little doubt about the uncertainties which exist. So, in the eastern tradition, initiation has continued as one unified rite which takes place generally in infancy; chrismation has not been separated out into a distinct rite of confirmation. In the West, confirmation has continued in the Roman Catholic tradition as a separate sacramental rite, but the link with the bishop has been partially severed; presbyteral confirmation is now an acceptable norm, using oil which has been episcopally consecrated. The widely acclaimed "Lima Document", *Baptism, Eucharist and Ministry* (hereafter the *B.E.M.*), does make brief explicit reference to confirmation. It notes:

> Christians differ in their understanding as to where the sign of the gift of the Spirit is to be focused. Different actions have become associated with the gifts of the Spirit. For some it is the water rite itself. For others, it is the anointing with chrism and/or the imposition of hands, which many churches call confirmation. For still others it is all three, as they see the Spirit operative throughout the rite. All agree that Christian baptism is in water and the Holy Spirit.[19]

In the Lima/*B.E.M.* commentary, there is a sharp note on this particular paragraph:

> If baptism, as incorporation into the body of Christ, points by its very nature to the eucharistic sharing of Christ's body and blood, the question arises as to how a further and separate rite can be interposed between baptism and admission to communion. Those churches which baptize children but refuse them a share in the eucharist before such a rite may wish to ponder whether they have fully appreciated and accepted the consequences of baptism.[20]

This diverts us, of course, along another path, that of communion before confirmation. It does, however, assume that confirmation itself is the "gateway" to communion. In the seventeenth century there was already a softening of this in the rubrics of the 1662 *Book of Common Prayer*, allowing for those who are ready and desirous to be confirmed to be admitted to communion. In the Church of England there is now widespread practice among the dioceses of admission to communion before confirmation. Such admission to communion need not undervalue nor undermine the theological foundations of confirmation, but rather open up the understanding of initiation as a process or an unfolding event. The following paragraph in the *B.E.M.* commentary hints itself at the lifelong nature of initiation:

> Baptism needs to be constantly reaffirmed. The most obvious form of such reaffirmation is the celebration of the eucharist. The renewal of baptismal vows may also take place during such occasions as the annual celebration of the paschal mystery or during the baptism of others.[21]

This reinforces again the need to place baptism in context as part of a more subtle and sophisticated understanding of the experience of initiation in the Christian life.

This approach has been rehearsed frequently within the Church of England over the past two decades. Both the report *On the Way* and the General Synod report on the same document helped set the context here.[22] These partly argued for a renewed commitment to a catechumenate, an approach already embraced since the Second Vatican Council by the Roman Catholic Church in its Rite of Christian Initiation of Adults (RCIA) process. Such a process both assumes that initiation is an unfolding event and also recaptures some of the keynotes of initiation from the early Church rooted in so-called mystagogical catechesis. *Common Worship* embraced much of this and the *Companion* notes that:

> ... the new provision ... places baptism as the theological centrepiece around which the rites of confirmation,

affirmation of baptismal faith and reception into communion
of the Church of England are clustered.[23]

Common Worship, then, abandoned the single rite of the *Alternative Service
Book* and opted instead for a *progression* of rites which also attempted
to reclaim some of the key catechetical insights of the early Christian
centuries. These reflections may assist us in gathering together what is often
seen as rather disparate material, as we seek to understand the theological
patterns which can reasonably be seen to underpin confirmation.

At the centre of the debate over confirmation lie issues of sacramentality
and the public affirmation of faith. Is confirmation a rite within which there
is a clear sense of God imparting grace, or is it instead an occasion when
an individual or a group of individuals publicly confess their faith and
commitment to Jesus Christ as Lord? This very sharp way of putting the
question leads itself to an inappropriate separation of these two essential
elements. To begin with, it assumes that confirmation cannot be both/
and. The *Companion*'s commentary on the shift between the 1549 and the
1552 Prayer Books, as we have noted, makes precisely this distinction.
Indeed, it is clear that this distinction was intended in the more radical
revisions of 1552. Although reference to the action of the Holy Spirit is
not lost, it is possible to argue that the revisions of 1552 do pull the rite
in a direction based more upon cognitive assent than upon sacramental
efficacy. There is no dispute over the fact of these changes and the intention
of some sort of shift of emphasis. There remains debate over whether
there is a deliberate intention, between 1549 and 1552, of moving from
an effective to a cognitive understanding. Revisionist understandings of
the history of the Reformation tend to reinforce the notion that a more
Protestant and less overtly sacramental interpretation was intended.[24]

The Reformers throughout Europe, in a multitude of different ways,
were keen to move from an apparent tradition of superstition to a tradition
where the word was proclaimed and where individuals thereby embraced
the faith in words, and not simply through an *effective* sacramental faith.
Individual confession of faith affected all aspects of the Church's life, from
worship to an appreciation of vocation or calling by God. This affected
not only the Reformed churches but also Roman Catholicism through

the Council of Trent. There too the direct voice of God to the individual would mark out vocation.

The rediscovery of initiation as an unfolding event, or as a pathway with key milestones, can bring together both these sets of insights, the sacramental and the verbal. In the early Church the pattern of setting out during Lent on a process of spiritual training took the candidates and the church community forward towards Passiontide, Holy Week, and Easter in a manner which embraced both the didactic and the sacramental, the intellectual and the doxological. Some, indeed, have argued that such a combined process reaches back into the Gospels and may indeed explain the shaping of the passion by the four evangelists. Did the passion narratives originate from teaching, worship, and an embryonic sacramental life lived out in the holy sites within Jerusalem? Putting aside such conjecture, we do know that such a tradition had developed by the fourth century with the pilgrimage patterns associated with Egeria.

Confirmation, then, should be understood as part of this larger unfolding pattern of initiation; that is, not as a crude "gateway" to communion, but instead as a sacramental and confessional milestone along the journey. Such an understanding has a number of merits. Across civilizations there has been a common tradition of some sort of maturity "rite of passage" which allows both the individual and the community to embrace this stage of development. It is there in the Jewish tradition of the *bar mitzvah*; it even developed in the atheistic culture of the former Soviet Union and its satellites.[25] This should not be seen as a means of validating the practice of confirmation, but rather as acknowledging this element within the rite. This relates directly to the affirmation or confession of faith, which also relates to the tradition of catechesis both in the early Church and as rediscovered since the Second Vatican Council. Such a process relates also to a sacramental understanding of the nature of confirmation within the broader pattern of an unfolding pattern of initiation. Confession of faith and an understanding of God's gracious action are not juxtaposed but are part of one and the same event. God's gracious act and our response lie at the heart of the baptismal covenant. Indeed, God's gracious act is frequently seen by Anglicans as one of the crucial reasons for the practice of infant baptism too. The laying on of hands and chrism stand alongside the decision and affirmation of faith

and not in contradistinction to each other. They also speak eloquently
for some candidates about an appropriate rite of passage.

In its introduction to baptism and the initiation rites, the Liturgical
Commission's commentary begins plainly with the affirmation:

> Baptism is the sacramental beginning of the Christian life.[26]

In itself this is a modest but significant claim. Just a few lines further
on it is stated more eloquently and within a clearer theological context:

> Those who are exploring the way of Christ for the first time
> set their feet on a path that leads to salvation.[27]

This is not to underplay the essential nature of baptism but rather to imply
that the journey in God begins here and effectively lasts a lifetime. It is
also sacramental and as such is an event, an action, and a liturgy which
does not solely relate to an individual, but to the individual's place within
the wider community, within the body of Christ. What does this say, if
anything, about the theological significance of the various unfolding
moments on the path to which baptism is the gateway and a clue to all
that follows? The beginnings of an answer may lie in the prayer which
was first introduced in the 1552 revision of the *Book of Common Prayer*
and which remained there in the 1559 and 1662 Prayer Books. It is the
prayer used at the laying on of hands:

> Defend, O Lord, this thy Child [*or* this thy Servant] with
> thy heavenly grace, that he may continue there for ever;
> and daily increase in thy Holy Spirit more and more, until
> he come into thy everlasting kingdom.[28]

There are two key elements in this prayer, which remains mandatory, but
is to be said by all after the laying on of hands in the *Common Worship*
order for confirmation. First of all, in a manner worthy of the Reformers,
the prayer begins with a direct reference to God's grace: "Defend, O Lord,
this thy Servant with thy heavenly grace . . . " Whatever the uncertainties
may be about the sacramental nature of the rite, the bishop calls for God's

grace to defend the person confirmed. In the *Common Worship* version it is in the plural. Then, secondly, we hear:

> . . . daily increase in your Holy Spirit more and more, until they come to your everlasting kingdom.

An emphasis on the continuing growth of the person (and so the Church) in grace is directly stated. This is further reinforced by the prayer interposed after this in 1552. Here then, in this Reformation rite, we encounter the notion of being "on the way", of this being part of a lifetime's journey continuing "until they come to your everlasting kingdom". Even the shift in the collect, from 1549 to 1552, to using the word "strengthen" suggests this sense of continuing growth in the Spirit. Might this offer us a clue to a theological understanding of confirmation and all that follows along the continuing journey?

—

Where have we got to so far, then? What are the key elements which we cannot ignore? First is a concern that Christian initiation should itself be missionary in its implications. So, for example, do our church buildings challenge people to understand the nature of the gospel simply by how they are ordered? Do font and altar point to entry and continuing nourishment? Then we are challenged to see how the rites themselves look outward to the community if they are to be embracingly missionary. This in itself requires initiation to be part of an unfolding event as indeed is human life itself. This leads us to place the different elements of initiation within a broader theological context which bursts the walls and boundaries which have unhelpfully constrained our understanding of baptism, confirmation, admission to communion, and indeed the Eucharist itself. The 1662 prayer with the laying on of hands at confirmation suggests a pattern of continuous growth in God throughout our lives. What might this mean about the imparting of grace or the reception of God as Holy Spirit through the initiation process and within the Eucharist? This also has further implications for our understanding of ordination.

It is easy to see confirmation and baptism as if their understanding and use have remained static. This is far from the truth, of course. So, the *Publick Baptism of Such as Are of Riper Years* entered the *Book of Common Prayer* only in 1662. The rite was deemed necessary following the years of the Commonwealth when infants had not been baptized. At times, confirmation was non-existent for Anglicans, when bishops were not resident or when Anglicans lived in colonies overseas. The pattern now often seen as the "norm", with bishops travelling round the diocese to confirm in parishes, is a Victorian development aided by the growth of the railways, turnpike roads, and the expansion in numbers of suffragan bishops. So first of all, then, patterns of initiation have changed. In recent years there has once again been a growth in the number of confirmations happening in cathedrals with larger numbers. This has largely been driven by theological concerns. Such confirmations emphasize the corporate element of the initiation rites; there is a clear sense of the Church at such occasions. Secondly, with imaginative use of cathedral buildings there can be an effective use of a staged rite. The rite of baptism occurs at the font, hopefully near to the church door. The entire congregation then moves on to the place of confirmation, perhaps at the crossing, if the cathedral is so designed. Finally, communion happens at the high altar, probably with the congregation standing as one body. The giving of the candle and "sending out" gives an opportunity for one more stage in the unfolding process of initiation. There is a third strand to such confirmations inasmuch as the bishop confirms in his church and may take the opportunity to spend a longer time with the candidates in catechesis, rehearsal, in some sort of social gathering, and finally in the baptism, confirmation, eucharistic rite itself.

Such an approach to the liturgy is also informed by the anthropological term "liminality". This refers to liminal experiences, threshold experiences, which relate both to "stages" in our life and to becoming part of a new community or group. Baptism and confirmation (and even the sending) are *liminal* moments in the life of the Christian believer. This is true, even with those who are baptized and/or confirmed but who remain on the margins of the Church.

What precisely, however, do we believe is going on theologically in the confirmation rite itself? Returning to an earlier point, we noted that baptism is the clue to all that follows. In any catechesis, this is the obvious place to begin. Byzantine fonts were designed to look like "walk-in" stone coffins near to the entrance of the church; the symbolism of dying and rising with Christ is clearly represented. Other images can be explored too: liberation and salvation, as with the Israelites being brought out of the water at the Red Sea; or cleansing as a sign of repentance and then turning again, as is made clear in the decision. These images also reinforce the experience of liminality. The waters of baptism are a powerful sacramental image and at the same time a proven catechetical impulse from which to begin. Bound up in the sacrament of initiation, however, are a number of different elements. Thomas Seville has helpfully set these out in an essay on confirmation. Seville makes it clear that baptism by water, from the earliest centuries, appears to have been accompanied by other signs, including the laying on of hands and the administering of oil in anointing.[29] There is a fairly clear consensus among many recent scholars that rebirth in the Spirit through the waters is operative in terms of a theology of salvation. One of the difficulties in the fragmentation of the rites of Christian initiation is that the different signs also become separated. This in itself easily leads to somewhat crude questions being asked about precisely what is happening alongside each of these sacramental signs—laying on of hands, anointing, dipping (or immersing and dipping) three times in water. Thus Seville points to similar difficulties in understanding the meaning of chrismation in confirmation.[30]

Seville's detailed analysis indicates how difficult it is to separate out different elements of the sacramental into separate "theological moments" within the different rites. All these different actions with water, oil, and laying on of hands are better seen as part of one organic whole. If that is the case, then the mistake is to attempt to focus God's action in the Holy Spirit at any specific moment within any of the rites. All of the signs are significant and important but they are not to be analysed such that God acts at one moment only. The *Companion to Common Worship* makes a helpful comparison here, noting:

> Much debate on ancient liturgical texts asks questions that our forbears in faith would not have asked and makes distinctions they would not consider. Just as today an

> Orthodox would not understand why you would ask
> whether the Spirit was conferred at water baptism or
> chrismation, so too the ancient writers of liturgical texts
> would not understand the question. It comes out of a
> Western interest in the "moment" of consecration. Rather
> they would affirm that the whole rite is both pneumatic and
> baptismal and the one cannot be divided from the other.[31]

The Western tradition has thus been much more concerned with instrumental questions which have tried to identify key sacramental actions with specific theological actions of God. If this mistake is avoided it opens up questions about the nature of baptism, confirmation, and the Eucharist in a far more fruitful and rich way. We can affirm God's grace as active in the Eucharist not simply immediately after the institution narrative, but as being effective through the celebration of the entire rite. So, too, we need to see baptism, confirmation, and the Eucharist holistically; the grace of God is made available in initiation throughout the unfolding event even when that event unfolds in a series of episodes which are sometimes chronologically fairly distinct from each other.

Perhaps at this point, however, it is worth noting one danger of seeing Christian initiation as an unfolding process. Such an understanding risks dissolving the concept of initiation into a notion of discipleship or more general understandings of participation in the life of faith. Whilst initiation into the mystery of the divine life is a life-long process, nonetheless there is, in the sense of initiation being discussed here, a focus upon the sacramental events that *begin* that process. That is, on the one hand there is a life of ongoing initiation and, on the other, events of initiation. In the same way that it is now proper to say that the whole eucharistic service is consecratory—and not one particular positivistically understood moment or set of words within that service—nevertheless it is *this* service at *this* time which is consecratory. As space- and time-bound creatures we do not have unmediated access to that which is universal and eternal. We understand such verities in and through events in time. In a world understood through the lens of the incarnation, it is the particular which mediates the universal. Thus it is that sacramental and efficacious *events* mediate to us the significance and meaning of what may be a process that takes more time, even a lifetime. The gift of grace, of course, can neither be commanded nor captured by any set of words, but it is always understood not as something general but as something both particular and personal. It is important that this understanding of the rites of initiation as efficacious *events* which signify for us that which takes place over longer periods of our lives is not lost.

So this understanding of Christian initiation—as an unfolding event signified by these particular events—opens up theological considerations on a broader front which again have been too easily constrained by an emphasis on a "moment of the Spirit" or, indeed, different moments of the Spirit, whilst also sometimes seeking qualitative differences in what the Spirit effects or transforms in these moments. In a very helpful passage Seville notes:

> In entering into the reality of Jesus Christ and His Church, the neophyte enters into a relation of participation with Jesus Christ and the Spirit, a share in the relation of the Son with the Father.[32]

This is an essential passage since it moves us from a rather fundamentalist form of pneumatology in Christian initiation to a full Trinitarian understanding, automatically implied by the threefold dipping and the threefold questioning at the decision. Even at this point there are real dangers. In the *Alternative Service Book*, the threefold decision opted for a form of modalism, separating out the Father as Creator, the Son as Redeemer, and the Spirit as Sanctifier. In *Common Worship* this is avoided by making all three questions turn around Christ as Saviour, as Lord, and as the way, the truth, and the life. In Pauline terms we are baptized into Christ, but this is to imply a full engagement with the life of God as Trinity.

As we try to regain a sense of Christian initiation as being a continuing initiation into and participation in the life of God, as efficaciously marked by sacramental events, we may be helped by recovering the use of a term more often encountered in the Eastern tradition: "perichoresis". The *Cyprus Statement* agreed by the International Commission for Anglican-Orthodox Theological Dialogue argues that the life of God is dynamic.

That is, God as eternally hospitable seeks to draw the believer into his life. So the terms Father, Son, and Holy Spirit:

> speak of identities that eternally constitute each other in their mutual relationships. Affirming the independent reality of the Spirit [as a Person, alongside the more obviously personal terms Father and Son] implies that the perfect love of Father and Son, the completeness of giving and receiving in God, is not all that should be said about the divine life. There is no exclusivity or mutual self-absorption in the relation of Father and Son, because there exists also the relation between the Father and the Spirit, and the Son and the Spirit. Thus God's life is a dynamic, eternal and unending movement of self-giving.[33]

However, because God is transcendent and "ever-more" than himself, this immanent life of self-giving also becomes "the free out-flowing of the Father's self-giving: in the economy of salvation the Holy Spirit offers us a share in the divine life to created beings."[34] God's life is offered for all and is that into which all are called to participate. It is the Spirit who takes us beyond any immanent self-contained Father-Son binitarianism in the Godhead and marks that openness in the Godhead, constituted by this mutual self-giving love, which invites the creature to share in God's life.

Perichoresis, then, with its understanding of mutuality and relationship within the Godhead, combined with concepts of *theosis* (or deification), gives a richer understanding of the Holy Spirit's interpenetration of the life of each individual human person. Through a spiritual process of adoption and filiation, the believer is caught up into the relationship which Christ shares with the Father (Romans 8. 15, 23 and Galatians 4. 6).[35] The Spirit forms the believer into the likeness of Christ (theosis). Indeed, just as the baptism of Jesus does not represent a moment of conversion but an "affirmation, through the Spirit, of Jesus' relation to the Father", which is his divine Sonship, so too the descent of the Spirit at baptism today marks the on-going process of filiation and deification in the life of the believer. As the *Cyprus Statement* puts it:

> [Jesus'] baptism is an initiation into the whole of his mission
> culminating in the cross [and so] baptism unites us with
> Christ in his death and resurrection (Romans 6. 1–11).
> At our baptism the Spirit forms Christ in us, and enables
> us to share in Christ's crucifixion and resurrection. Then
> we begin to live in the Spirit . . . because the liberation of
> our humanity for life among God's people, accomplished
> in Jesus' death and resurrection, becomes a reality in us.[36]

These concepts of perichoresis, deification, and filiation may help us appreciate better the relationship between the intellectual, spiritual, and liturgical in relation to Christian initiation, as the believer is caught up into the life of God within the Church. Such an understanding also helps avoid the fragmentation of theological discourse to which the Western tradition has been prone and which the Caroline Fathers did much to repair;[37] the Caroline tradition rediscovered the integral nature of theology bringing doctrinal, moral, and ascetic reflection together as one. Entering into Christ through the whole process of initiation implies a turning from sin, an entering into a living relationship with God in worship—a relationship which the processions of the divine Trinity exhibit—and a reshaping of our lives in God. The Caroline Fathers similarly saw ascetic, doctrinal, and moral theology as all of a piece.

The Western tradition has by no means been entirely devoid of this continuous perichoretic theological understanding. We were reminded of it two generations ago by Charles Williams, especially in his book *The Descent of the Dove*, and indeed more widely, in his re-capturing of the use of the term "co-inherence".[38] Williams develops the term co-inherence, which in the tradition is often used synonymously with perichoresis, in a number of sophisticated and interrelated patterns. So in an incarnational and participatory mode it draws together spirit and matter. Thus he notes of the Alexandrian school:

> Yet there is about them a sense of the *naturalness* of
> Christianity, as distinguished from its catastrophic
> supernaturalness.[39]

In his postscript to *The Descent of the Dove*, Williams develops this further in relation to the Church and its place in the world. This relationship of Church to world is made especially clear in the rites of initiation. At baptism, godparents stand for the candidate in his or her worldliness and naturalness. It is brought together in confirmation:

> It is this co-inherence which, at the confirmation, he [the candidate] confesses and ratifies.[40]

For Williams, however, such ratification is not a purely intellectual assent. Instead it implies too the fullness of the indwelling Spirit of God by means of which all co-inheres. This co-inherence or perichoresis, then, proceeds from God in Trinity and binds together spirit and matter, human and divine. The sacramental rites in their totality mirror and make effective such co-inherence in the life of the individual believer and of the Church of God as it lives for the world.

Rather more recently, Gavin Ashenden, bringing this together in his study of Charles Williams, writes as follows:

> The habitual tendency in Christian theology to separate spirit and matter has diverted religious and visionary energy from the practicalities of much of everyday life. The secular has been stripped of the sacred and the energy for renewal and transformation that the sacred carried with it . . . Williams's philosophical and theological healing of the division yields two consequences. Each of them has the capacity for transformation.[41]

The two consequences include "a theological vision for the integration of matter and spirit."[42] Later he notes:

> Williams's vision of co-inherence provides the justification for linking the progress of the human condition perceived in classical theological terms with the need for social and political transformation.[43]

Part of Christian initiation and the journey which it implies is just such a transformation. Seen as an unfolding series of episodes with the grace of God continuing but still focused in sacramental acts, baptism, confirmation, the affirmation of faith, and a eucharistically centred life offer a realistic opportunity for transformation. Ultimately this takes us full circle to those two separated communities on the north-western edge of that Yorkshire town and within that ancient university. Our vision of Christian initiation needs to be able to bring them together. It is God co-inherent in humanity and nothing less that is offered.[44]

NOTES

1. First published as "The rites of Christian initiation—a bishop's theological reflections on liturgical practice", in *The Journey of Christian Initiation: Theological and Pastoral Perspectives* (by members of the Faith and Order Commission of the General Synod of the Church of England), pp. 106–125 (Church House Publishing, 2011, ISBN 9780715142370), and reproduced here by kind permission of the publisher (<https://www.chpublishing.co.uk>).

2. Cf. Wesley Carr, *Brief Encounters* (SPCK, 1985), especially Chapter 5. Carr makes some important points about the relationship of pastoral practice to a theoretical ecclesiology.

3. The House of Bishops has authorized less direct questions to be used, as in the *Alternative Service Book*. See *Common Worship: Christian Initiation* (Church House Publishing, 2006), pp. 112 & 168.

4. David Thompson, *Baptism, Church and Society in Modern Britain: From the Evangelical Revival to "Baptism, Eucharist and Ministry"* (Paternoster, 2005), p. xvi.

5. Jeremy Morris, FOAG Paper, CCU/FO/07/20, p. 4.

6. *Common Worship: Christian Initiation*, p. 319 (emphasis added).

7. Presumably the separation of the baptism from the main Eucharist derived from an unease in the congregation at having large numbers of baptisms regularly in their main weekly worship; some would also argue that such a

public setting is also difficult for families who are not regularly part of the church family.

8. In the Collect the wording changes: in the 1549 Prayer Book the third phrase runs, "send down from heaven, we beseech thee, (O Lord) upon them thy Holy Ghost the comforter, with the manifold gifts of grace; the spirit of wisdom and understanding . . . " In 1552 this changes to "strengthen them, we beseech thee, (O Lord) with the Holy Ghost the comforter, and daily increase in them thy manifold gifts of grace, the spirit of wisdom and understanding . . . " There is a shift towards the cognitive from the effective through the emphasis on the gradual increasing of the gifts of the Spirit both in the Collect and in the newly interposed following prayer. The signing of the cross and the prayer that goes with it are removed in 1552. There is a clear reference in 1549 to confirming and strengthening candidates with the inward unction of the Holy Ghost. Once again the removal of this, alongside the insertion of the new material in 1552, reduces the stronger sense of sacramentality implied in 1549. This shift in emphasis is confirmed by Geoffrey Cuming in his *A History of Anglican Liturgy* (Macmillan, 1969), pp. 86–87. He notes of 1549, "Confirmation is literally translated from the Sarum rite, with the one alteration that anointing is replaced by laying-on of hands, with a reference to 'the inward unction of the Holy Ghost'; signing with the cross is kept. The service ends with the greatly shortened version of the prayer in Hermann's *Deliberatio*, one of the very few Orders to have a confirmation service at all. Cranmer is obviously copying Hermann's arrangement of the whole section, beginning with an introduction headed 'Confirmation, wherein is contained a Catechism for children', in which Hermann's influence is clearly apparent, then printing the Catechism, and finally the actual service of Confirmation. He also agrees with Hermann in giving up the use of oil and introducing the laying-on of hands." Cuming goes on to say of the 1552 rite, "In Confirmation, however, the signing with the cross and its prayer are removed; and God is asked, not to send down the Holy Spirit upon the candidates, but merely to strengthen them with him. The laying-on of hands is accompanied by a new prayer based on Hermann." (p. 113).

9. Paul Bradshaw (ed.), *A Companion to Common Worship* Vol. 1 (SPCK, 2001), p. 158. This commentary is what it says it is and has the authority as of those who produced it; it is not the "official teaching" of the Church of England.

10. "Christian Initiation: Birth and Growth in Christian Society" (CIO, 1971).

11. This followed a tradition established in the 1948 and 1958 Lambeth Conferences and by the 1948 report, *The Theology of Christian Initiation*, and the 1958 Church of England Liturgical Commission Report, *Baptism and Confirmation*.

12. See "Christian Initiation as a Whole Process (Is baptism 'complete sacramental initiation'?)", FOAG Paper, CCU/FO/05/33 [A revised version of a paper offered to the Fifth Meissen Theological Conference], and also, more recently still, "Is baptism 'complete sacramental initiation'?", in *Theology* Vol. 111 Issue 861 (May/June 2008), pp. 163–169.

13. Avis, "Is baptism 'complete sacramental initiation'?", p. 163.

14. Bradshaw (ed.), *A Companion to Common Worship*, p. 174.

15. Some would argue the chrism is not given full theological significance in the *Common Worship* rite, since it remains optional.

16. Bradshaw (ed.), *A Companion to Common Worship*, p. 178.

17. Avis, "Is baptism 'complete sacramental initiation'?", p. 168.

18. Ibid., p. 169.

19. *Baptism, Eucharist and Ministry* (World Council of Churches, 1982), Faith and Order Paper No. 111, p. 5, paragraph IV B 14. Available online (<http://www.anglicancommunion.org/media/102580/lima_document.pdf>).

20. Ibid., p. 5 (*Commentary*, 14 (b)).

21. Ibid., p. 5 (*Commentary*, 14 (c)).

22. *On the Way: Towards an Integrated Approach to Christian Initiation* (Church House Publishing, 1995). Cf. also Bradshaw (ed.), *A Companion to Common Worship*, p. 161.

23. Bradshaw (ed.), *A Companion to Common Worship*, p. 161.

24. For general background here see Diairmaid MacCulloch, *Tudor Church Militant* (Penguin, 1999), and also Diairmaid MacCulloch, *Thomas Cranmer: A Life* (Yale University Press, 1998).

25. James Thrower, *Marxism-Leninism as the Civil Religion of Soviet Society: God's Commissar* (Edwin Mellen Press, 1992), Studies in Religion and Society Vol. 30.

26. *Common Worship: Christian Initiation*, p. 325.

27. Ibid.

28. *The Book of Common Prayer* (Oxford University Press, 1662), "Order of Confirmation".

29. Thomas Seville CR, "Confirmation" (unpublished paper).

30. Seville, "Confirmation", pp. 11, 13–14.

31. Bradshaw (ed.), *A Companion to Common Worship*, pp. 175–176.

32. Seville, "Confirmation", p. 17.

33. *The Church of the Triune God: The Cyprus Statement agreed by the International Commission for Anglican-Orthodox Theological Dialogue* (The Anglican Communion Office, 2006), pp. 26, II. 5. Available online (<http://www.anglicancommunion.org/media/103818/The-Church-of-the-Triune-God.pdf>).

34. *The Cyprus Statement*, pp. 26, II. 5.

35. Ibid., pp. 26, II. 6.

36. Ibid., pp. 36, II. 40.

37. Henry McAdoo makes this point in analysing the Caroline tradition in his *The Structure of Caroline Moral Theology* (Longmans, Green, 1949). See especially Chapter VI. Here McAdoo argues for the unity of moral and ascetic theology and for this as an integrating structure for all theological disclosure.

38. Charles Williams, *The Descent of the Dove: A Short History of the Holy Spirit in the Church* (Longmans, 1939). See also particularly his essay "The Way of Exchange", in *"The Image of The City" and Other Essays* (Oxford University Press, 1958).

39. Williams, *The Descent of the Dove*, p. 37 (emphasis original). See also Paul L. Gavrilyuk, "The Retrieval of Deification: How a Once-Despised Archaism Became an Ecumenical Desideratum", in *Modern Theology* 25: 4 (October 2009), pp. 647–659. Gavrilyuk's discussion of a recent interest in deification perhaps shows that Charles Williams' own work on this (from an earlier generation) is now reflected in a broader ecumenical trend for which themes of *theosis*, coinherence, and perichoresis are important. This is part of a wider retrieval of Christian Platonism, which tradition is already well-represented in Anglicanism, for example in the persons of the Cambridge Platonists such as Ralph Cudworth. Some would also argue that the influence on Anglicanism can be traced back to the conciliarists and notably to the thought of Nicholas of Cusa.

40. Williams, *The Descent of the Dove*, pp. 234–235.

41. Gavin Ashenden, *Charles Williams: Alchemy and Integration* (Kent State University Press, 2008), p. 233.

42. Ibid.

43. Williams, *The Descent of the Dove*, p. 234.

44. I am grateful to the Revd Dr Paul Avis and Dr Martin Davie for helpful comments on the text, and to the Revd Dr Matthew Bullimore for some help in the initial research for the paper and for later comments.

4.   A THEORY OF LITURGICAL RELATIVITY[1]

Unquestionably there are many candidates who might be considered for "the prize for the greatest influence of all over the twentieth century", either for good or for evil. Whoever might win that competition, undoubtedly Dr Albert Einstein would be in the last six, if not the all-out winner. His "Special" and "General" Theories of Relativity have helped shape our world in so many different ways. Within the compass of his writings, the famous equation $E=mc^2$ would take pride of place. In this tiny arrangement of formulae is encapsulated a remarkable revolution in our understanding of the universe. For within this compact mathematical expression we find energy, mass, and light all brought into conjunction with each other. So no longer are the physical world around us, or the energy which enlivens and powers that world, or indeed time itself independent and unchanging qualities. All are relativized and effectively we cannot understand any one of these standing alone. None loses its significance but instead the importance of each is enhanced, but only if taken in conjunction with the other two. Einstein's equation has helped redefine our understanding of reality, with a significant impact upon our capabilities both scientifically and in how we order our lives.

Scientific relativity might seem an unlikely place from which to start a brief reflection on our understanding of Christian liturgy within human experience. Nevertheless, a variety of different influences have come together to cause something similar to the relativizing revolution in science to occur within liturgical studies. Only a generation ago, liturgy was practised largely as a historically comparative study. For Anglicans this often meant a detailed analysis of how the 1662 *Book of Common Prayer*

came to arrive in its present form. Often a rather superficial understanding
of the progress of the English Reformation led to a deterministic description
of the process which helped form the 1559 Elizabethan prayer book.
Throughout the twentieth century, however, the application of a more
objective scholarly critical historical apparatus began to have its impact.
Dom Gregory Dix's classical study of the Eucharist is one outstanding
example of this.[2] This study itself, however, needs to be placed within the
wider context of the development of the Liturgical Movement, notably
the work of Dom Lambert Beauduin at the monastery of Mont César
in Louvain, and then also the work of Abbot Ildefons Herwegen and
Dom Odo Casel in the monastery of Maria Laach in the Rheinland.[3]
Increasingly, liturgical study proceeded within an ecumenical context,
and by the last quarter of the twentieth century this became explicitly so
in the publication of composite volumes cataloguing the largely growing
consensus in scholarship.[4] This process itself brought with it positive
ecclesiological implications.

These implications were spelt out in practice through the liturgical
revision which was a common part of the history of almost all the
mainstream churches in the last decades of the twentieth century. The
advent of the Second Vatican Council inaugurated by Pope John XXIII
in 1960 by a *motu proprio* furthered the process of liturgical revision
dramatically. The Constitution on the Sacred Liturgy was promulgated
at the end of the second session of the Council in December 1963.[5] The
direct result of this was the publication of the *Missa Normativa*, a modern
language rite published simultaneously in several languages. Overnight
the liturgy was to be in the vernacular in each of the local churches across
the world. Indeed, if Latin was to be used at all, then once again it must
be the "normative rite", and the Tridentine Mass became illegal, leading
to the celebrated rebellion of the Lefebvrists. Within other churches, too,
liturgical revision proceeded apace. In the Church of England, a Liturgical
Commission was established, which in 1965 produced a report offering to
the Church Assembly a new series of rites, the *Alternative Services: Second
Series*.[6] In 1967 the Convocations of Canterbury and York authorized
these services for experimental use for a period of four years.[7] At the
same time the Convocations authorized for permissive use, for a period
not exceeding seven years, the *Alternative Services: First Series*.[8] These

were the rites produced for the "deposited" 1928 *Book of Common Prayer* which Parliament had refused to authorize at that time. Later, following further revision and indeed, by this time, synodical debate, the revised rites were brought together in the *Alternative Service Book*.[9] In the year 2000, following still more radical revision, the main corpus of *Common Worship* was authorized and published for use.[10] A similar history could be catalogued for most mainstream Christian churches during this period throughout the world.

The process of revision in itself, then, produced a relativization of Christian liturgy. Often one heard people reflecting, "I went to their service and it was virtually the same as ours!" That observation still comes from Methodists attending Anglican liturgies, Anglicans attending Roman Catholic Masses, and so on. This relativization has been accompanied in its impact by another aspect of liturgical study and practice. Through the study of liturgy in the context of *time*, through a renewed understanding of *liturgical space*, and perforce (through ecumenical developments) the study of worship and *community*, the process of relativization has proceeded in a more sophisticated sense. For each of these key factors is an essential element within the liturgy which in itself cannot be described without taking into account all these three factors. Now, however, they are seen as three relating variables. They are the equivalent of a liturgical $E=mc^2$. We can see this quite sharply by reflecting on three recent studies, which themselves form just one strand within a wider process of relativization within liturgical scholarship. These three pieces of scholarship issue from quite different points of origin but they serve to illustrate this process of both clarification and relativization. Relativization, it should be noted, is not used here pejoratively but descriptively; it does not advert to a reduction in objectivity. Let us then use three quite different monographs to reflect further upon this liturgically relativizing revolution.

—

Beginning with time, amongst these three variables, let us use Pink Dandelion's analysis of Quaker liturgies as an illuminating point of departure.[11] To speak of liturgies in the context of Quakerism sounds to be almost an oxymoron, but Dandelion makes a good case for understanding the situation so. Beginning with the minimalist arrangements of the Meeting House, he sets out, in an introduction, to illustrate the key part played by time in the developing and varying styles of Quaker liturgy, over the past four centuries. At the heart of these developments are changes in the assumed eschatological context. Dandelion contrasts Quaker liturgy with Church liturgy and, indeed, the foreword to his analysis is written by an Anglo-Catholic. In his first chapter Dandelion expands on the theme of time, particularly in relation to the "end of time". The eschatological landscape is plotted frequently in the book by means of diagrams which juxtapose creation, the first coming, and the second coming. As the context is set, so he points too to the incidence of early Quaker millennarianism. The second coming of Christ, however, was, for Quakers, an "inward experience" and marked the beginning of the end of the world.[12] The scene-setting for this owes much to George Fox himself, the founder of the Society of Friends, who encouraged his followers to move out of an obsession with conventional calendrical time. The stress, then, is upon our inward Christianity, rooted in a covenant of *light* rather than in the more common Puritan covenant of grace. This offers the possibility of collective intimacy with God outside calendrical time.

Dandelion then moves on to examine the essential part of silence in Quaker worship. Time itself is transformed in the use of silence. The Friends, of course, prescinded from developing sacraments and so understood "ordination" as a "setting apart" of the entire community.[13] The relationship of heaven and earth is thus established for Quakers and is reflected in their worship; biblical references (Zephaniah 1. 7 and Ecclesiastes 5. 2) are used to support this, and particularly to support the centrality of silence. This leads Dandelion to a discussion indicating how Quakers are called to transcend the limits of worldliness. Nevertheless, despite this call to a proper "un-worldliness", Quaker eschatology begins to be modified even as early as the late seventeenth century; the end-time recedes. Also from these early times, Quaker worship developed differently in relation to specific worshipping communities and different geographical locations. These variations included both distinctive dress and the "intoning" of those ministries offered within the silence of worship. Both these facets of worship lend strength to the use of the term "liturgy" within Quakerism.

Having examined a variety of different approaches to life and worship amongst the Friends in the eighteenth and nineteenth centuries, Dandelion moves into the present day again, describing the variety of approaches to worship and contrasting *evangelical, conservative,* and *liberal* meetings.[14] In the liberal tradition theistic belief is by no means universal. Out of this liberal tradition issues an optimistic view of human nature and the emergence of Matthew Fox's concept of original blessing in contrast to original sin.[15] Dandelion concludes his analysis by coming full circle and returning explicitly to questions of liturgy and time. Again, this needs to be understood from within the context of differing traditions within the Society of Friends. In his concluding reflections on what he describes as liberal-liberal Quakerism he notes, "[Silent] worship is generally not understood in traditionally Quaker ways, even whilst some are still engaged in a personal relationship with a God who gathers and guides. It is seen as a method equivalent to other church forms where the theological underpinning is marginal compared with the experience possible in the silence."[16] Dandelion's analysis, then, indicates the determinative part played by time in Quaker worship, and this is ultimately set in a postmodern context both in terms of theology and the variety of different Quaker communities. Both *time* and *space* are essential parameters within worship, as indeed is *community,* but there are marked differences with the broader sacramental tradition of both eastern and western Christianity.

———

The minimalist arrangement and the use of space within Quakerism contrasts sharply with the often complex and varied use of space within sacramental Christianity. The concept of sacred space has been examined in some detail in recent monographs. Philip Sheldrake has looked broadly at the importance of sacred space.[17] John Inge focuses sharply on the understanding of sacred space within the Christian tradition.[18] Alongside these two very useful studies stands Kevin Seasoltz's comprehensive discussion of space in conjunction with Christian art, architecture, and theology.[19] The sheer scope of this work means, inevitably, that some elements are discussed in greater detail than are others. The starting point here is an historical analysis dividing culture into primal, classical, modern, and post-modern eras. Seasoltz then uses these criteria to see how the churches have responded to these culture shifts. Liturgy, Seasoltz argues, is part of the attempt by Christians to live life in God as encountered in Jesus Christ. He believes that liturgy exists primarily to show a vision of what life, understood in the Christian context, is really about. From this starting point he suggests that the development of Christian architecture is as important as the development of theology itself.[20] Picking up two of the three concepts we have described in the relativization of liturgy, he notes, " . . . *time* and *space* are the two most basic categories used to analyze culture, for they tend to be the fundamental perceptions in which people cast and interpret reality."[21]

His analysis continues with reflections upon understandings of sacred space in the Old and New Testaments, and also in the early Church, before he moves on to the Post-Constantinian period. The emergence of the basilican pattern at this point was, of course, seminal. During this period there was also an important development in sacred images, culminating in the use of icons and iconic representations. Seasoltz then shifts directly from the Byzantine age to the Romanesque and Gothic periods. He emphasizes the importance of the Rule of St Benedict and the flowering of the monasteries in the development of architecture and the use of sacred space. This architectural shift was accompanied by an associated development in the Church's understanding of the Eucharist which contrasts with the understanding in apostolic times. He writes, "Strongly influenced by the teaching of St Isidore of Seville, the Romanesque church emphasised the significance of the eucharist as the great gift of divinity which God grants men and women and which descends on the altar at the consecration of the Mass."[22] Seasoltz's discussion of the Renaissance, Baroque, and Reformation periods is equally, if not more, illuminating with regard to our understanding of the developing interplay between architectural and theological principles. The movement from the stylized iconography of the Byzantine period into the three-dimensional art of Giotto and the Renaissance painters is a key turning point in his argument. Later he speaks admiringly of Cranmer's contribution to liturgical prose, but also indicates how developing Reformed theology changed the shape and use of buildings and so of sacred space.[23] One might also make reference at this point to the work of Diarmaid MacCulloch, notably in his work on Cranmer and on the Reformation more widely.[24] MacCulloch indicates, in his historical analysis, the increasingly Protestant nature of Cranmer's theology and its impact upon his liturgical revisionism. This view of the development within Cranmer's theological understanding needs to be placed alongside Seasoltz's own appreciation of Cranmer's contribution to liturgical expression.

As he continues his analysis within the seventeenth, eighteenth, and nineteenth centuries, Seasoltz is interesting in his reflections on the ironies of Pugin's influence. Pugin was adamant that the Roman Catholic Church was the only true church and that its faith is best expressed through the sacred space of Catholic architecture. His impact on Roman Catholicism, however, was insignificant in comparison with his influence on the Tractarian movement within the Church of England.[25] This analysis is followed by a key chapter in which Seasoltz discusses the birth of the Liturgical Movement in the work of Dom Lambert Beauduin at Louvain and Ildefons Herwegen and Odo Casel at Maria Laach. This work, of course, preceded the changes that would emerge from Vatican II. Throughout the discussion, Seasoltz engages with theology, architecture, and sacred space, concluding his survey with the work of Le Corbusier and the modernists. In the chapter which deals with the twentieth century, he indicates how architectural principles have explicitly been brought into play in the re-ordering of church buildings. He is interesting, for example, in his discussion of the merits and failings of both theology and architecture in the cathedrals at Coventry, Liverpool (notably the Metropolitan Cathedral), Clifton, and Brentwood.[26] In the final chapters of this book, Seasoltz examines a number of church buildings, analyzing how effectively theological principles have been applied in the design or re-ordering of a variety of different churches, some secular and some monastic. The argument here elaborates on these same themes. The choice of buildings, which is to some degree idiosyncratic, and is based specifically on Seasoltz's own preferences and knowledge of particular buildings in Europe and North America, nevertheless illustrates the key argument very effectively. So despite this deliberate eclecticism, his conclusion that sacred art and architecture should act as *loci theologici* places space at the very heart of liturgical relativity. He notes within his conclusion, "It is above all God's Spirit in our hearts and communities that gives us access to the otherness, the transcendence, the holiness of God."[27]

———

These words bring us, then, to our final variable, that of community. Here the work of Martin Stringer helps focus the argument. This key element of community within the liturgy stands central to Stringer's sociological analysis of the development of Christian worship.[28] Stringer argues from the very beginning that the crucial issue here is a sociological rather than a cultural history of worship. Stringer sets out in some detail and clarity his own methodology. He does this both at the beginning of his main argument and by recapitulating it at the start of other chapters throughout the book. By this process, he makes it abundantly clear what he is and what he is not intending to achieve. So Stringer looks at worship using the analytical category of the *discourse*, and indeed what he describes as "discourse communities". He achieves his aims by dividing Christian history into seven three-hundred-year sections. In his first section, concluding at AD 300, he points to the increasing institutionalization of worship and so to the marginalizing of ecstatic approaches such as those encountered in the Pauline context.

The second period, up to AD 600, is about the colonization of sacred space in the Roman Empire. This colonization occurs differently in Jerusalem, Rome, and Constantinople, but it does nevertheless happen in *each* place.[29] Employing another sociological term, Stringer talks of "hegemonic discourses" in the years from 600 to 900. Worship is now used to protect traditions that are under threat and, on occasion (as in fourth-century Armenia), this led to the emergence of the "Christian state". Again varying traditions emerge, and are protected differently in contrasting parts of the later Byzantine world.

In the next period, up until 1200, Stringer argues that the *dominant* discourse of Christianity is established. That dominant discourse is reinforced or structured by worship.[30] From this emerge different Christian cosmologies. In the period from 1200 to 1500 we encounter another sociological category, that of the "demotic discourse"; here devotion and liturgy, superstition and worship are contrasted. It would be interesting to place this distinction alongside Eamon Duffy's recent study of the devotional use of "Books of Hours" by the laity in the mediaeval period.[31]

In the penultimate period, Stringer introduces the rise of "humanistic discourses", where the focus shifts (even within the Christian churches) from God to the human person. He argues that this is not a process of "de-Christianization" or "secularization" but instead of humanistic discourses now becoming dominant, as did the Christian discourse in the period from 900 to 1200.[32] Finally, the period from 1800 to 2000 marks the globalization of Christian worship.

Stringer's analysis offers crucial tools in understanding the development of Christian worship, and notably the place of the community in this development. The text is precise and methodologically based. The conclusion refers to us looking for too much comfort in our church buildings and being too tame in embracing varieties of style. Nonetheless, Stringer offers an excellent analysis of the importance of the community as the basis of worship and Christian liturgy. He is also challenging in arguing for new and different developments of liturgy in the contemporary context.

—

Alongside the work of Dandelion and Seasoltz, and indeed relating to much other recent research, Stringer's study reinforces the threefold elements in the relativization of the liturgy. Sacred space, time, and community now form part of one single equation which describes the nature of Christian worship and the place of liturgy within a wider theological analysis. This suggests a significant shift in our understanding of liturgy and of the theology which underpins it. This also moves us a long way from archaeological textual analysis and historical comparative study. The importance of these remains, but they are part of a broader and more complex narrative. So these three analyses and the more substantive development in liturgical scholarship reinforce the significance of the context for liturgy, and of liturgy for the shape of Christian belief. Orthodoxy and Anglicanism, in particular, have always embraced the *lex orandi, lex credendi* tradition: doctrine issues from worship. Nonetheless, this tenet is a necessary but not a sufficient condition for the emergence of a full ecclesiology. Achieving a proper balance between space, time, and community within the liturgical equation will undoubtedly help safeguard the key part that worship should play in developing both a balanced theology and ecclesiology. Worship, however, cannot be the only deciding factor and the process of relativization rather reinforces this point. In this process of relativization, however, we see the developmental or even evolutionary nature of Christian belief. We see also the key part which worship and liturgy play within the life of Christian discipleship: relativity here refers not to *relativization,* but instead to the way in which space, time, and community are essentials in understanding both Christian worship and Christian faith, and need to be understood as relating to each other as part of a greater whole.

NOTES

1. First published as "A Theory of Liturgical Relativity", in *Ecclesiology* Vol. 5 No. 2 (2009), pp. 237–245, ISSN 1744–1366, by Brill Academic Publishers; reproduced here by kind permission of the publisher (<https://www.brill.com>). A version was also presented as the Alcuin Club Lecture for 2007.

2. Gregory Dix, *The Shape of the Liturgy* (A&C Black, Dacre Press, 1945).

3. R. Kevin Seasoltz, *A Sense of the Sacred* (Continuum, 2005); see particularly pp. 229–245 and p. 394.

4. See, for example, Cheslyn Jones, Geoffrey Wainwright, and Edward Yarnold SJ, *The Study of Liturgy,* (SPCK, 1978).

5. Austin Flannery OP (ed.), *Vatican Council II: The Conciliar and Post Conciliar Documents* (Costello Publishing, 1975, 1987); "The Constitution on the Sacred Liturgy", pp. 1–282.

6. The Church of England Liturgical Commission, *Alternative Services: Second Series* (SPCK, 1965).

7. So, for example, *An Order for Holy Communion* (SPCK, 1967).

8. See again, for example, *Alternative Services: First Series. An Order for the Administration of the Lord's Supper or Holy Communion* (SPCK, 1967).

9. *The Alternative Service Book* (SPCK, 1988).

10. *Common Worship: Services and Prayers for the Church of England* (Church House Publishing, 2000).

11. Pink Dandelion, *The Liturgies of Quakerism* (Ashgate, 2004), pp. 4ff. Dandelion establishes time (and, indeed, space) as key concepts within Quaker worship.

12. Ibid., p. 12.

13. Ibid., p. 28.

14. Ibid., pp. 82ff.

15. Ibid., p. 95.

16. Ibid., p. 126.

17. Philip Sheldrake, *Spaces for the Sacred: Place, Memory and Identity* (SCM Press, 2001).

18. John Inge, *A Christian Theology of Space* (Ashgate, 2003).

19. Seasoltz, *A Sense of the Sacred*, pp. 55f.

20. Ibid., pp. 64f.

21. Ibid., p. 68 (emphasis added).

22. Ibid., p.122.

23. Ibid., pp. 166ff.

24. Diarmaid MacCulloch, *Thomas Cranmer: A Life* (Yale University Press, 1996) and *Reformation: Europe's House Divided, 1490–1700* (Penguin, 2004).

25. See also Rosemary Hill, *God's Architect: Pugin and the Building of Romantic Britain* (Penguin, 2008).

26. Seasoltz, *A Sense of the Sacred*, pp. 262ff.

27. Ibid., p. 344.

28. Martin D. Stringer, *A Sociological History of Christian Worship* (Cambridge University Press, 2005), p. 9.

29. Ibid., pp. 64ff.

30. Ibid., p. 120.

31. Eamon Duffy, *Marking the Hours: English People and Their Prayers, 1240–1570* (Yale University Press, 2006).

32. Stringer, *A Sociological History of Christian Worship*, pp. 181f.

5. RE-ANIMATING SACRIFICE?[1]

The title of this chapter may seem enigmatic, even to the level of perversity. Does not the term "re-animate" raise many of the problems that have caused sacrifice to become such a fraught concept? Does it not suggest a separated sense of the soul which reflects a crude Cartesian analysis, hints of a "ghost in the machine" driven out two generations ago by the philosopher Gilbert Ryle and others? Does it not still more dangerously hint at animistic religion and even animal sacrifice? Such practices are never entirely banished from our sophisticated theological world: only four years ago, during a visit to the remarkable cathedral at Alaverdi in eastern Georgia, the visitor was accosted by a sign marked with an arrow, "Animal sacrifices this way", pointing round to the side of the perimeter wall of the cathedral precincts; it suggested that, for some, the message of the "new covenant" in Jesus Christ, set out classically in the Letter to the Hebrews but hinted at elsewhere in the New Testament, has still not taken root. But the title is deliberately ambiguous and we shall return to it later. Suffice to say that sacrifice is an essential element, still, in Anglican eucharistic thought and practice, as we shall discover.

The direction this chapter follows was originally given through a providential impulse. As I sat down to write, the Roman Catholic weekly *The Tablet* published a brief but incisive article by Philip McCosker, stimulated initially by Pope Benedict's homily in Westminster Cathedral during his visit to Britain in September 2010. Not unexpectedly, it made reference to the child-abuse controversy, but alongside this, it adverted to the issue of sacrifice in the Eucharist. Summarizing part of the Pope's reflection, McCosker wrote:

> Our worship is inscribed and patterned by the inner
> Trinitarian dynamic. We offer our sacrifice of praise and
> thanksgiving to God, empowered and drawn up by the Spirit
> into the Trinitarian life of self-offering: the self-gift of the
> Father in the revelation of the Son, and the Son's self-gift
> to the Father in the Spirit.[2]

Here we encounter, as we shall see later in this analysis, almost a
classical description of the Anglican (or at least the Church of England's)
understanding of sacrifice within the Eucharist. McCosker's contribution
also implicitly introduces (and notably through his references to Sarah
Coakley's writings) other key elements in relation to sacrifice in the
Eucharist and more widely within Christian theology. This surfaces,
in particular, with reference to the writings of René Girard where his
theology touches profoundly upon a description of "Christ's death as an
innocent scapegoat".[3]

This reminds us of a key issue relating to the language of sacrifice.
Sacrifice may be seen broadly in either a strong or a weak sense. A *strong*
understanding of sacrifice does indeed return us to various forms of
animist religion and to certain Old Testament strands of the theology
issuing from ancient Judaism. Here, animal sacrifices are made in order
to propitiate gods (or Yahweh), often with the intention of restoring the
relationship between a tribe, a nation, or the whole of humanity, and the
god (or gods) who are worshipped. Presumably this is what continues in
some manner at Alaverdi in eastern Georgia. Similarly, the tiny surviving
Samaritan sect who still worship on Mount Gerizim in Palestine continue
to sacrifice lambs. The *weaker* sense of sacrifice (and sometimes it is very
weak) is a description of individuals or communities giving something
up, or offering something as an earnest of their devotion to God. So,
for example, churches throughout the world still appeal to adherents
for "sacrificial giving" to God so that the finances of the institution may
prosper. Rarely does such sacrifice ever begin to impinge seriously on
the life of the giver in the manner described in the Gospel narrative of
the widow's mite.[4]

In relation to the Eucharist, the various meanings of sacrifice were
explored in a classic essay by Leslie Houlden during the early 1960s, in

relation to liturgical renewal in the Church of England. He is clear that some associations of sacrifice, which relate it to propitiation of wrathful gods, are now for us effectively dead metaphors; they no longer relate to our experiences. His essay makes it clear that a simple polarization of sacrifice into the two patterns described above is in itself too facile. So he writes, "the term has covered a wide variety of ideas, many of them having hardly any relation to each other and operating along quite distinct theological lines."[5] Furthermore, this is complicated by the plethora of different understandings of atonement to which sacrifice may refer, so, "There are, for instance, many christologies, many doctrines of the atonement. But in the case of eucharistic sacrifice, it is accentuated by uncertainty as to which precisely is at stake."[6] Houlden points forward to the key question of how the Eucharist relates to atonement and soteriology more generally. So, for example, is the eucharistic narrative about *re-presentation* or *representation*? This was a crucial topic for the sixteenth-century Reformers. Sarah Coakley notes that for Luther, in his "Babylonian Captivity", eucharistic *sacrifice* was the third captivity alongside the restriction of the chalice to clergy and transubstantiation, and it was "by far the most wicked of all."[7]

Alongside Houlden, Coakley also points to a variety of different ways of understanding sacrifice. These include the offering of a victim, destruction, division, substitution, commensality (eating together), apotropaism (warding off divine wrath), and moral self-giving.[8] Thus the range extends from bloody violent sacrifice to the commanding heights of human altruism. It was precisely in this area that the most heated debates about eucharistic sacrifice raged during the Reformation period. The Church of England as an institution emerged from these conflicts, and Thomas Cranmer, Archbishop of Canterbury during the reign of King Henry VIII, Edward VI, and also Queen Mary, is an interesting indicator of how the Reformation developed. Cranmer began as a moderate Protestant but shifted to become a more determined and radical Reformer, as Diarmaid MacCulloch has demonstrated so clearly.[9] We can see this shift taking place as the eucharistic liturgy developed in the two Prayer Books of King Edward VI in 1549 and 1552.

In the 1549 rite, the eucharistic prayer remains an integrated whole, as we now (within almost all traditions) would recognize it: the preface, the institution narrative, and then the anamnesis are continuous. Even here, however, Cranmer makes a significant shift. All mention of sacrifice is moved back so that it comes after both the preface and the narrative of institution. Although the 1549 rite retains the Sarum shape, all the offertory prayers—with their strong sacrificial language—are removed. Sacrifice remains, but it has already become a post-communion thanksgiving. No longer do believers offer themselves to God in the perfect offering of Christ made present in the Eucharist. Now it is the reception of the sacrament, the memorial enacted, that *strengthens* these to offer themselves to God in Christ and thus to make themselves available for his *service*, so it runs, "rendering unto thee most hearty thanks, for the innumerable benefits procured unto us by the same, entirely desiring thy fatherly goodness, mercifully to accept this our Sacrifice of praise and thanksgiving, most humbly beseeching thee to grant, that by the merits and death of thy son Jesus Christ, and through faith in his blood, we and all thy whole church, may obtain remission of our sins and all other benefits of his passion. And here we offer and present unto thee (O Lord) ourselves, our souls, and bodies to be a reasonable, holy, and lively sacrifice unto thee."[10]

So the language of sacrifice remains, but its theological gravitas has been transformed into one of thanksgiving and memorial. In 1552, things are moved on a stage further. Now the eucharistic prayer is fragmented into three. The preface comes first and thereafter, now separated off by the "Prayer of Humble Access", we encounter the institution narrative; finally comes the communion of the people. It is only after this that we encounter the language of sacrifice, this time in what became known as the "Prayer of Oblation". Now the separation from the eucharistic action is complete, although still the language of sacrifice is retained. The "reasonable, holy and lively sacrifice" is still there as we offer "ourselves, our souls and bodies". There, too, is the clear reference to the "Sacrifice of praise and thanksgiving".[11] In the eucharistic prayer there remains a strong emphasis on Christ's sacrifice being "the one oblation of himself once offered . . . full, perfect, sufficient . . . " It is interesting that in both prayer books, "Sacrifice" here remains capitalized. The key, then, was to retain the sacrifice of praise and thanksgiving, the reasonable, holy, and lively sacrifice, and the offering of ourselves, our souls, and bodies, but to make it crystal clear that this was not a crude repetition of the perfect sacrifice of our Lord. This was the key to the Reformers' concerns. It must be a theology of representation and not re-presentation.

———

This area of ground has been very carefully debated and analysed during the past "ecumenical century" and also during the parallel process of liturgical and eucharistic renewal. Nevertheless, as recently as the 1970s, mainstream Anglican theologians were keen to safeguard the Reformation revisions. In an essay of exemplary clarity, Professor Richard Hanson offers a critical analysis of the issues. Starting with the Old Testament, he examines the patristic witness of Justin, Hippolytus, and Irenaeus. But it is Cyprian, for Hanson, who makes the unthinkable leap of the Eucharist becoming "the offering of Christ by the celebrant" ("president" in modern parlance). He writes, "When we turn to consider the eucharistic offering in Cyprian we find that he has made just that move which we have found virtually all our authors hitherto stopping short of. He unequivocally regards the eucharist as an offering of Christ by the celebrant."[12] One of the by-products of Cyprian's theological development is a strongly sacerdotal view of the priesthood. In a revised version of his essay, Hanson argues that three currents of intellectual development came together to form a single core of spiritual and intellectual doctrine in the Middle Ages and during the Counter-Reformation. These three were the concept of "offering" developed by Cyprian, the "realistic" doctrine of the consecration of the bread and wine, and a newly emergent sacramental understanding of episcopacy and priesthood. Hanson notes that this combination formed a powerful core: " . . . this was the decisive factor in the evolution of the Christian clergy into a separate hierarchical body who were in some respects exempt from secular control or legislation and tended to form a kind of state within a state."[13]

At the end of his fairly sharp and excoriating critique of these developments, however, Hanson returns to the doctrine of eucharistic sacrifice. He notes that the early Christians, from the author of the *Didache* onwards, linked their concept of sacrifice to their worship in the Eucharist: "They held that in the eucharist we offer thanksgiving and praise and prayer to God in Christ indeed, but that we also there offer

ourselves, our souls and bodies, our intentions and wills and works."[14] In
his concluding section Hanson argues that sacrifice is something given
graciously *by* God and not something which humanity offers *to* God, so,
"In this view, the eucharist becomes what its very early name implied,
above all an occasion of thanksgiving, with which are united of course
communion in Christ and our offering of ourselves in Christ to God";[15]
that is, participation in Christ.

In some ways, Hanson's reflections mark a late outpouring of some of
the arguments rehearsed in the four centuries following the Reformation.
There remain some sharp corners in his argument and it does not present
a complete and integrated expression of Anglican understandings of
eucharistic sacrifice. This is picked up summarily by Rowan Williams in
another classic essay on the subject. Towards the end of his essay Williams
notes, "With many of the criticisms levelled by Professor Hanson against
certain ways of talking about the eucharist and their practical and 'political'
consequences, I am in entire sympathy; but I do not believe that he (or,
indeed, other critics of sacrificial imagery) has told the whole story."[16] So,
for example, Williams demurs at the over-simplistic dichotomy between the
manward and godward outlined in Hanson's essay.[17] He does, however, at
the beginning of his article accept that certain views of sacrifice have indeed
been responsible for the development of a hierarchical and separated view
of sacerdotal priesthood.[18] He also accepts that some Catholic defenders
of sacrificial language have equally caricatured Reformed theologians as
rooting all salvation as a "long-term effect of an event in the past". This,
he argues, is a parody of Calvin and others.

Williams, in a parallel manner to Hanson, examines the patristic
evidence but engages with others including St Ignatius of Antioch. He also
brings alongside this the Syrian tradition. He argues, too, that both Richard
Hanson and Robert Daly[19] are too bald in their summary of Irenaeus. In
Irenaeus' talk of sacrifice being a "necessity", there are implications that
sacrifice is a natural ritual expression of grateful love. That is, there is a
link between the earthly offering of praise and the eternal "liturgy" of
the Trinity. This, too, undermines a simplistic human-godward contrast
implied by Hanson. Later again, in exploring the image of "the altar in
heaven", Williams argues that we are returned to "the idea of the eucharist
as a celebration of God's gratuitous love".[20] In bringing together Ignatius'

association of the Eucharist with Christ's sacrificial death and Ephrem the Syrian's image of Christ sacrificing himself, Williams moves us away from sterile arguments about *repeated* sacrifices and then returns us to the Anglican tradition in Cranmer. He is prepared to accept the unsatisfactory nature of restricting the thanksgiving to the post-communion, but argues that in present scholarship the centrality of thanksgiving is fairly universally accepted. One should note that thanksgiving is still present in the opening dialogue and at the beginning of the preface, as it was in Sarum. In his concluding section Williams writes, " . . . the eucharist was a *memorial* of an event which increasingly gathered to itself sacrificial metaphors."[21] It is the coming together of these two concepts of memorial and sacrifice which has helped us understand better a rich Anglican pattern of thought relating to eucharistic sacrifice. This is a movement which has also been at the heart of ecumenical convergence on this subject.

—

Towards the end of his analysis of sacrifice in the Eucharist, Leslie Houlden reflects thus:

> For whenever God acts in the cause of bringing men to true relationship with himself, he acts unreservedly as himself and exhibits always the same dependable characteristics; whether in the person of Jesus or in the sacrament of the eucharist or in any facet of the work of his grace.[22]

It is precisely the sense of continuity in soteriology and salvation history captured by Houlden that has enabled us to rediscover the true resonances of eucharist and sacrifice which have been the fruits of ecumenical endeavour. For this reason, if one were seeking a model or definitive summary of an Anglican understanding of eucharistic sacrifice, then an obvious starting point would be the agreed statement on the Eucharist issuing from the Anglican-Roman Catholic International Commission. It may seem odd to start from an ecumenical document until one reflects on the nature of the process which was embarked upon in ARCIC in such a pioneering manner. Nowhere is this process better summarized than in

Pope John Paul II's words to the members of ARCIC I at Castel Gandolfo. Fascinatingly, he begins by dwelling upon sacrifice:

> I greet you with honour, veterans, seasoned workers in a great cause—that unity for which Christ prayed so solemnly on the eve of his sacrificial death . . . Your method has been to go behind the habit of thought and expression born and nourished in enmity and controversy, to scrutinise together the great common treasure, to clothe it in a language at once traditional and expressive of the insights of an age which no longer glories in strife but seeks to come together in listening to the quiet voice of the Spirit.[23]

ARCIC, then, goes behind the sixteenth-century controversies to seek out a common tradition.

—

This brings us to a tantalizing realization. So often Christians are asked to seek out distinctivenesses. What is distinctive about Franciscan or Benedictine spirituality? What is the distinctiveness of an Anglican or Roman Catholic understanding of eucharistic sacrifice? Often, attempting to answer such questions can feel like chasing moonbeams or pursuing an impossible mercurial act. Of course, there are nuances in all theological reflections, but the exercise in which we have been engaged thus far is something which we all share, as the late Holy Father hinted in those words. ARCIC speaks for both Anglican and Roman Catholic theologians. Its method is the same as that pursued in this brief chapter. How do the ARCIC documents bring together the reflections with which we have engaged?

In the *Final Report* of ARCIC I, it is made plain that there can be no repetition or addition to what was accomplished once for all in Christ's death. Christ's sacrifice is given the currency and continuity implied in Houlden's essay[24] by the use of the word "memorial", which is itself seen as a translation of the Greek word "*anamnesis*". In using this Greek root, memorial does not imply simply bringing to mind a past event, as one might do at an act of remembrance following a war or similar catastrophe.

Instead the Eucharist embraces "the church's effectual proclamation of God's mighty acts. Christ instituted the eucharist as a memorial (*anamnesis*) of the totality of God's reconciling action in him. In the eucharistic prayer the church continues to make a perpetual memorial of Christ's death, and his members, united with God and one another, give thanks for all his mercies, entreat the benefits of his passion on behalf of the whole church, participate in these benefits and enter into the movement of his self-offering."[25] The Commission was criticized for its use of *anamnesis* and in its later elucidation it expands its own logic, tracing usage of this word both to the New Testament and to Justin Martyr. The elucidation restates the logic and then adds, "In the celebration of the memorial, Christ in the Holy Spirit unites his people with himself in a sacramental way so that the Church enters into the movement of his self-offering. In consequence, even though the Church is active in this celebration, this adds nothing to the efficacy of Christ's sacrifice upon the cross, because the action is itself the fruit of this sacrifice."[26]

In its 1991 response to the *Final Report* the Roman Catholic Church asked for greater clarification on some specific issues. This included questions about the relationship of the eucharistic memorial to the *once-for-all* sacrifice of Calvary and about "the propitiatory nature of the eucharistic sacrifice, which can be applied also to the deceased". The Commission responded to this in the document *Clarifications* (published in 1994). Again, on the first point, the Commission re-affirms and re-states the logic behind its use of the term memorial, meaning *anamnesis*. On the propitiatory nature of the eucharistic sacrifice it is made clear that the 1662 *Book of Common Prayer* emphasizes propitiation, God's favour towards us, both in the prayer of consecration and in the later prayer of oblation. The use of the phrase "we and *all thy whole church*" in the prayer of oblation allows for the commemoration of the departed to be a continuing part of Anglican liturgical practice.[27] These "Clarifications" provoked a nervous and even hostile response amongst some Anglican evangelicals, but Charles Sherlock, an Australian Anglican with evangelical roots, responded subtly and positively in a later essay. In a careful analysis, Sherlock separates out sacrifice, atonement, and propitiation. He argues that propitiation is about love and not revenge or appeasement. He concludes, further, that by the sixteenth century the distinction between sacrifice and atonement had become completely blurred. He notes:

> Cranmer makes the (Protestant) point that Christ's one, perfect, sufficient sacrifice is complete, but [in the so-called "Comfortable Words"] he invites worshippers to look to heaven where Christ our Advocate is the (still living) propitiation![28]

In two key sentences, Sherlock concludes, "*Clarifications* is distinctive, I would thus argue, in that it carefully separates these senses, and so sets forward the dialogue in the divided Western church. It thus offers considerable hope to liturgists and theologians alike, especially those 'conservatives' who take with full seriousness notions such as propitiation in respect of the work of Christ."[29]

———

Sherlock's helpful analysis, with his affirmation that propitiation is about love and not vengeance or appeasement, returns us both to our title and the starting point of this essay. In Philip McCosker's reflections on Pope Benedict's emphasis on the eucharistic sacrifice, McCosker's main starting point is a remarkable inaugural lecture by Professor Sarah Coakley which might be described as one of the most recent contributions to Anglican thinking about sacrifice and the Eucharist. There is insufficient space within the scope of this chapter to rehearse her entire argument, but it is important to sketch the skeleton of her reflections. *Pace* Sherlock, Coakley argues that much recent late-twentieth-century writing on sacrifice has been negative, focusing on violence and irrationality; René Girard, she argues, is a notable culprit. Propitiation in his thought is not about love. Secondly, she argues, there has been a wider diffidence about rationality in Christian theology. Where rationality has been defended, it has often been marked by a retreat into a closely defended theological compound, safe from the ravages of the natural and social sciences. Finally, she draws upon insights from evolutionary biology, including Charles Darwin, from which she believes Christian theology can receive a proper confidence in contributing to the wider debate about belief, and about human motivation more generally.

In this brief response to her work, theology and rationality form a good starting point. Coakley cites a variety of different writers who she believes too easily capitulate or retreat into a dangerously decreasing area of debate, defended against other disciplines by deliberately not engaging with a wider world of converse and dialogue. One of the failings is the assumption that eighteenth-century Enlightenment discussions of rationality can only take the theologian down the road to various forms of deism: she notes some examples. However, such views of rationality were not the only response. Samuel Taylor Coleridge offered, during that same period, and through his "polar logic", a far more nuanced and confident theological approach to reason and rationality which is able to engage effectively with the narrative and imagery of the Christian tradition, including sacrificial language.[30] Moving from here to Coakley's concern about Girard and others, she argues that their emphasis on a violent *mimesis* plays into the hands of those aggressive atheists who deplore the irrationality and destructive potential of religion. Furthermore, Coakley is not convinced that Girard's later adjustments to his earlier theory carry weight.

Now undoubtedly *mimesis* is at the heart of liturgical theology and its performative practice.[31] Mimesis underpins both the Old and New Testament witness and also stands central to the rehearsing of the *mystery* of the Christian faith in the Eucharist. This understanding of mystery refers to the appropriate re-presentation of the great and mighty works of God seen in the life, passion, death, and resurrection of Jesus. This is the crux of the liturgical theology of Odo Casel,[32] and receives a new impetus in Coakley's use of evolutionary understandings of sacrifice. Quoting Charles Darwin in *The Descent of Man* (1871), she reminds us, "There can be no doubt that a tribe including many members who, from possessing in a high degree the spirit of patriotism, fidelity, obedience, courage, and sympathy, were always ready to aid one another, and to sacrifice themselves for the common good, would be victorious over most other tribes; and *this would be natural selection*."[33] Coakley's argument is that, far from allowing Christianity to become defensive or to go into retreat, this suggests that the pattern offered as a *mimetic* foundation (my words) in Christian theology, rooted in the narrative of the life, ministry, passion, death, and resurrection of Christ, could hardly be a more positive foundation for humanity. Darwin underscores the key concept of sacrifice. Lest one might assume that this implies a rather weak and even sentimental altruism, one only needs to point to the witness of someone like Maximilian Kolbe (and other similar examples) to see the power of such a positive sacrificial mimesis rooted, of course, in Jesus Christ and rehearsed daily in the eucharistic action. Kolbe and others gave their lives after the pattern of Christ. Furthermore, it does not need to be underpinned by a violent or vindictive theology of atonement. There are many contemporary models which offer other analogies and images. So Melanie Klein's theory of "projective identification", where a patient/client projects the worst of themselves on to the counsellor who then holds it, but is able to hand it back without its characteristic destructiveness,[34] is just one such model which can be applied to the sacrifice of Christ and, indeed, the entire narrative of his life.

This argument, then, takes Coakley's insights and argues for an Anglican understanding of eucharistic sacrifice which not only embraces the ecumenical accord seen in the ARCIC dialogue and rooted in the history of Anglican theology, but offers it in a renewed form to suggest a confidence in Christian theology and worship. It is a confidence which offers to nurture humanity through what F. C. Burkitt described almost a century ago as "logical sacrifice". It is a re-animating sacrifice, a sacrifice which gives life in and through God and so it is also sacrifice re-animated.

NOTES

1. First published as "Reanimating Sacrifice?", in *Theology* Vol. 115 No. 1 (January/February 2012), pp. 26–35, ISSN 0040571X; reproduced here by kind permission of Sage Publishing (<https://uk.sagepub.com>).

2. Philip McCosker, "Sacrifice Regained", in *The Tablet* (16 October 2010), p. 6.

3. Ibid., p. 7.

4. Mark 12. 41ff. and parallels.

5. J. L. Houlden, *Explorations in Theology 3* (SCM Press, 1978), p. 65.

6. Ibid., p. 66.

7. Sarah Coakley, "Sacrifice Regained: Reconsidering the Rationality of Christian Belief", Inaugural Lecture as Norris-Hulse Professor of Divinity at the University of Cambridge, 13 October 2009, (Cambridge University Press, 2012), p. 10.

8. Ibid., p. 9.

9. Diarmaid MacCulloch, *Thomas Cranmer: A Life* (Yale University Press, 1996).

10. *The First and Second Prayer Books of Edward VI* with an Introduction by Professor J. R. Porter (Prayer Book Society, 1999, a re-issue of the earlier Dent Everyman edition), p. 223. [N.B. Language transliterated into modern English for the sake of comprehension.]

11. Ibid., pp. 389–390.

12. R. P. C. Hanson, *Eucharistic Offering in the Early Church* (Grove Books, 1976, 1979), p. 17.

13. Ibid., p. 24.

14. Ibid., p. 27.

15. Ibid., p. 29.

16. Rowan Williams, *Eucharistic Sacrifice: The Roots of a Metaphor* (Grove Books, 1982), p. 32.

17. See note 12 above.

18. Williams, *Eucharistic Sacrifice*, p. 4. See also Richard Gaillardetz, *Ecclesiology for a Global Church: A People Called and Sent* (Orbis Books, 2008).

19. Robert J. Daly SJ, *The Origins of the Christian Doctrine of Sacrifice* (Fortress Press, 1978), pp. 104–110 (on Philo).

20. Ibid., p. 16.

21. Ibid., p. 31 (emphasis added).

22. Houlden, *Explorations in Theology 3*.

23. Edward Yarnold SJ, *They are in Earnest: Christian Unity in the Statements of Paul VI, John Paul I, John Paul II* (St Paul Publications, 1982).

24. See note 18 above.

25. *Anglican-Roman Catholic International Commission: The Final Report* (Catholic Truth Society/SPCK, 1982), p. 14. Available online (<http://www.anglicancommunion.org/media/105260/final_report_arcic_1.pdf>).

26. Ibid., p. 20.

27. Anglican-Roman Catholic International Commission, *Clarifications on Eucharist and Ministry* (Church House Publishing/Catholic Truth Society, for the Anglican Consultative Council and the Pontifical Council for Promoting

Christian Unity, 1994), pp. 5–6. Available online (<https://iarccum.org/doc/?d=19>).

28. Charles Sherlock, "Eucharist, Sacrifice and Atonement: The 'Clarifications' of ARCIC", in David R. Holeton (ed.), *Our Thanks and Praise: The Eucharist in Anglicanism Today* (Anglican Book Centre, 1998), p. 127.

29. Ibid.

30. Cf. Stephen Platten, "One intellectual breeze: Coleridge and a new apologetic", in *Theology* Vol. 111 Issue 863 (September/October 2008), pp. 323–335, and also Douglas Hedley, *Coleridge, Philosophy and Religion: Aids to Reflection and the Mirror of the Spirit* (Cambridge University Press, 2000).

31. Cf. Stephen Platten, "Liturgical Living: Learning by Mimesis", in *Anaphora* Vol. 5 No. 1 (June 2011), pp. 23–38, and also in this volume, Chapter 7.

32. George Guiver, *Pursuing the Mystery: Worship and Daily Life as Presences of God* (SPCK, 1996), and cf. Odo Casel, ed. Burkhard Neunheuser, *The Mystery of Christian Worship and Other Writings* (Newman Press and Darton, Longman and Todd, 1962).

33. Coakley, "Sacrifice Regained", p. 21.

34. See, for example, Stephen Platten and John Sharpe, "Christ—Holding Humanity in God?", in *Theology* Vol. 92 Issue 746 (March 1989), pp. 113–120.

6. THE BIBLE, SYMBOLISM AND LITURGY[1]

To speak of anything is a matter of relative simplicity, until we allow ourselves to become self-conscious about it. Once that point is reached, every word potentially becomes charged with complexity. Philosophical cats, for example, are notorious for sitting upon alternating idealistic and realistic mats, depending upon the time of day at which one calls. God-talk is not immune to such problems; indeed, here language is stretched to its very limits. Religious language is unavoidably analogical. This is a necessary truth forced upon us by the definition of our terms. God is necessary, humanity is contingent, hence, in philosophical terms, there is an epistemic distance separating humanity from God. Any attempts, then, that we make to speak of God and his relationship with us will force us back upon analogy. Symbol, image, model, and myth are not evils to be pruned out like dying twigs, but are rather the foliage which covers the growth. Such foliage is vital to life, although change it surely will as year succeeds to year.

Symbolism and images become more central still to religious discourse when we move to the area of liturgy, for here they seek not merely to describe the divine, but to evoke the response of awe and worship. This crucial significance of imagery in worship, however, allows us no suspension of our critical awareness. Instead it requires us to sharpen our analytical tools.

To begin with, then, what exactly do we mean by symbolism? Edwyn Bevan's classical definition is perhaps helpful. He distinguishes between two forms of symbol.[2] The first includes such diverse examples as the flag and the cloud of incense. Each of these holds significance within its own sphere, but conveys no new information about that sphere. The second form of symbol, and here the definition springs from A. N. Whitehead, elicits consciousness of other components of expression within the human mind. New patterns of thought and new inter-relationships are suggested through the impulses generated by the image. It is with this type of symbol that we shall be concerned here, notably in the use of images within liturgy.

Now in this tortuous but necessary preamble, nowhere yet has Holy Scripture been mentioned. However, within theology, and especially liturgical theology, Scripture operates little differently as *text* from the way in which religious language is used elsewhere; it is instead a specific case in point. Revelation in Holy Scripture, as elsewhere, is perceived through the operation of images. This process was made most explicit in a particularly sophisticated manner in Austin Farrer's seminal Bampton Lectures, *The Glass of Vision*. The Bible is a great wellspring from which pours forth a flood of images, some specific, some universal. So for Farrer, the shadow of the infinite is found in the finite, but without devaluing the finite person through whom all this is made possible.[3] The natural is raised up to perform a supernatural act and, by this means, certain images communicate the divine.

The richness of Farrer's thought lies particularly in two insights. The first of these has been hinted at already. It is of the nature of an image that it must bear relationship to what is already familiar to us, and yet be able to develop our perception and understanding further. This lies central to the theory of analogy. If an image is alien to all of our earlier experience it will remain meaningless and impotent, part of an arid academic exercise. "And what are atoms really like?" asks the twelve-year-old child. "They are like the plants in the solar systems of distant nebulae," comes the eloquent reply, and the child sits in stunned silence, with an air of mystified dumbness. The image, attractive as it might sound, does not move the listener on or broaden her perception. Farrer's second crucial argument is that religious images are irreducible. In his own words:

> . . . analogy is the proper form of metaphysical thought, in
> the realm of *thought* there is no getting behind it.[4]

The existent reality behind the image may be different from our perception thereof, but the images remain irreducible and they are as far as we are permitted to travel toward the divine consciousness. The Bible is redolent with material which bears witness to these insights. The Jews pictured Yahweh in images taken from their own experience. Yahweh was like a great king, Yahweh's salvation was the deliverance of a nation, Yahweh's power was such that, when he spoke, the earth trembled. So, for example, if we assume the enthronement psalms to have been rooted in some form of liturgy,[5] then the images come tumbling out to serve the needs of worshippers:

> The Lord reigneth; let the earth rejoice;
>   let the multitude of the isles be glad.
> Clouds and darkness are round about him;
>   righteousness and judgement are
>   the foundation of his throne.
> A fire goeth before him
>   and burneth up his adversaries round about.
> His lightnings lightened the world;
>   the earth saw and trembled.
> The hills melted like wax at the presence of the Lord,
>   at the presence of the Lord of the whole
>   earth. (Psalm 97. 1–5, RV)

Even within these few lines it is possible to discern images of varying importance. Some would retain greater universality than others. Kingship was a principal image in Israel, lightning and melting wax subsidiary and less central. Farrer notes that the principal images act as canons of control over the lesser images. Hence, presumably, Passover, Exodus, and kingship will determine to some extent the currency and appropriateness of less central images. Furthermore, Farrer notes, no images, however archetypal, should become idols. For him, the central significance of the incarnation will prevent such a mistake from occurring. That is part of the crux of his argument.

Farrer's approach to biblical revelation was arguably the most effective excursion into this area within twentieth-century hermeneutics. It combines reflection upon biblical religious thought with a general theory of religious language. Even this theory, however, is not without its difficulties. The first and most obvious problem is the apparently God-given nature of *certain* images. Whilst we may perceive something of the divine through such linguistic symbolism, it is not a great step from Farrer's notion to seeing these symbols as inviolable, indeed almost as extensions of the Godhead. Like a many-tentacled octopus, God reaches out into selected, but *only* selected, symbolic spheres of life. Clearly this will not do as it stands. The arbitrary nature of many images, their limited life, and subsequent death must lead us to see them as the product of God-with-man; that is, we cannot assume that they are ultimately God-given and beyond question. This leads to a second point of uncertainty with Farrer's argument. In his sophisticated efforts to avoid a fundamentalism derivative of a propositional view of revelation, Farrer could be accused of falling into the trap of a fundamentalism of biblical images. At certain points in his argument this certainly is a danger. So at one stage he compares biblical "poetry" with that of the post-Renaissance poets. For such writers it is but the stuff of life which moulds their images. For such as Jeremiah, however (and, we assume, for most biblical writers):

> . . . what constrains *his* images is the particular self-fulfilling
> will of God, perceptible in the external events of history
> and nature which God controls, perceptible also in a direct
> impact upon Jeremiah's inspired mind.[6]

And yet, despite this special treatment given to biblical images and their being raised above ultimate criticism, Farrer *does* appear to admit that images are born, reborn, and die. The Incarnation is the final destination, and some images will be rejected and others change their nature as the journey towards that most primary image continues.[7] Biblical images do occupy a unique place within the tradition but they cannot stand entirely outside similar canons of criticism as would be applied to all other symbols.

Now these caveats should make it clear that only a modified Farrerian theory can carry the weight which he would have wished it to carry—Farrer almost seems to imply such modification in his own self-critique. Adopting such a notion can allow us to move into a more general discussion of the use of images in liturgy. There is, however, one further insight of Farrer's which can be developed as we continue with this critique. It relates to the nature of poetic disclosure. Such disclosure has the ability to draw upon a very wide symbolic canvas. Farrer writes:

> The phrase which is just right has infinite overtones: or it awakens echoes in all the hidden caves of our minds.[8]

Hence it is true to say that through the careful and precise choice of a particular phrase, we arrive at a deliberate poetic non-precision. The right image will evoke response within us over a wide range of human experience. The poetic will draw together thoughts which evaporate once reduced to more supposedly objective forms of thought. As when light hits its prism at exactly the right spot, colours are refracted and dispersed in many directions, so is our thought refracted through the prismatic effects of any aptly chosen image.

But such precision will require great care from us in the use of images. Consistency will be vital. To mix images, or to use the same images in different ways within the text, invites opaqueness and confusion. So once again, it is essential that appropriate images are used. An image which is appropriate at one particular time and place may well lose its power completely, if transferred without reflection. Images will change, be criticized, and sometimes, later, die. But who will adjudicate upon such issues? Again this cannot be sanctioned by God. Instead, the human mind engages with this process through God's grace. Often the process will be haphazard. The refiner's fire which assists in the purification of images will vary greatly. At times, it will have been the linguistic creativity of an individual: Thomas Cranmer is but one example; at other times it may be the work of a liturgical commission, sometimes it may be through a Council of the Church, and on other occasions liturgists may marshal the talents of a modern poet. In the end the judge will be posterity, although posterity has a bad name for inconstancy. Ultimately, images will have been born and died, they will sometimes have been reborn and recast, but none has literally a divine right to immortality unless it is related to the primary beliefs which shape the Christian message. Austin Farrer saw the force of all this, but there remained the danger of allowing biblical images to become absolutized in a manner that his own argument itself ruled out. Nonetheless, his essential theory for the mediation of religious truth offers much, both in the use of scriptural images and also in later images developed within the tradition.

Biblical imagery is still subject to critical usage, and this is equally true of its use in liturgy. It is to examples of the application of such canons that we shall now turn. Let us focus upon just two prisms often used in worship. How do these prisms scatter the colours, and have we always been using the best glass?

—

Food, medics and psychologists remind us, is a primary human need. This discovery is hardly remarkable and surely stands behind what is one of the central images in Christian liturgy, that of bread. So the loaf, the wafer, or host, is the supreme focus in the Christian Eucharist. It speaks to us of our dependence upon food for life, of bread to sustain, but it suggests far more than this. As light floods through our symbolic prism, colours scatter widely. The bread becomes spiritual food, the death of Jesus is flashed through our mind, the sharing of the loaf at the Last Supper is there, the broken body, and so too the shared unity of a common meal. It could well be that this breath of symbolism was not there from the first. Central though it may have lain within the tradition, the Last Supper quite possibly stood originally as a common meal. Be that as it may, however, the sophistication of developing Christologies would soon transmute the shared bread of a common meal into an image which would communicate a profound wealth of spiritual realities.[9]

Given the development of bread imagery within the Eucharist, then, probably its crucial power lies in the visual plane. Bread is there to be seen. Sometimes in modern liturgies an actual loaf is used; it is carried up by a member of the worshipping community. It is taken by the priest, blessed and broken, and the people feed. The staple diet of the people lies at the centre of that liturgy which is the trademark of the Christian community, the Eucharist. But how do we, as a community, handle such precious imagery? To answer this question, let us take as a sample liturgy three of the Eucharistic Prayers from the Church of England's *Common*

Worship Order One Eucharist.[10] It will serve as well or as ill as any other modern rite and is a useful quarry on account of its clear biblical roots. In this brief analysis let us confine ourselves to four points, where biblical quotation is obvious.

At the centre of the eucharistic canon in Prayers A, B, and C lies this institution narrative:

> . . . who in the same night that he was betrayed,
> took bread and gave you thanks;
> he broke it and gave it to his disciples, saying:
> Take, eat; this is my body which is given for you;
> do this in remembrance of me.

As with its elegant predecessor, Thomas Cranmer's *Book of Common Prayer*, this narrative of institution is a conflation of Pauline and synoptic material. The sources are 1 Corinthians 11. 24 and Matthew 26. 26 (and its parallel, Mark 14. 22). Now it is generally agreed that this narrative has come down to us in two fairly different redactions. Those of Paul and Luke bear similarities, while over against these are those of Matthew and Mark. The contrast often made here is between Palestinian and Hellenistic traditions, although consensus is less than clear here.[11] Presumably in both accounts we are to think of the body of Jesus about to be offered upon the cross, and this is supported by commentators on the Pauline text, notably the phrase "*to huper humon*".[12] Hence in both texts, Pauline and Matthean, it seems legitimate to see a linking of the two images of feeding and deliverance. In Paul, however, it is impossible to separate these meanings from Paul's other imagery of the body, notably in his model of the Church. This is specifically taken up by Paul in the previous chapter, in 1 Corinthians 10. 17. Here, as C. K. Barrett indicates, there is virtually no doubt that the body refers to the Church, since Paul will use the term *sarx* for the flesh of Christ's human body.[13] Hence, in the Pauline interpretation (1 Corinthians 11. 24), the nuances are various, the prism gives us at least three different colours. Our mind is directed towards deliverance, feeding, and the Church.

Now the Matthean text does not yield a parallel image of the Church, except by reading Paul back into Matthew. Matthew's image of the Church is far less dynamic and organic. For Matthew, the Church is pictured instead as the ark[14] with the disciples as its model crew. It is, at most, an embryonic ecclesiology reflecting a community still bounded by Judaism and the law, to some degree, in contrast to developed Pauline thought.

To merge these two narrative strands, then, may present the danger of desecrating both edifices, Pauline and Matthean. On the experiential level it may also be a recipe for confusion. To mix such different images will paint a picture where the style and even content stand in contrast to each other. It may even blur the images. In other words, to expand the scientific parallel, images should scatter colours over a spectrum, rather than produce interference patterns with dark bands. Images are there to be evocative, to enlighten, and not to confuse. Simply to criticize *Cranmer's* approach would be mistaken. Much of the tradition within his work goes back well before the Reformation. Furthermore, contemporary scholarship and the critical method have highlighted the varying theologies held within the different biblical strands issuing from the various writers. But to ignore these insights can blur the clarity of the text. Nowhere is this more true than with the use of imagery.

A second quotation from the text presses the point home. At the fraction in the same rite, all join to say:

> Though we are many, we are one body,
> because we all share in one bread.

It is a direct quotation from 1 Corinthians 10. 17, a verse which we have already placed under scrutiny. The Pauline notion of the Church as the body of Christ is clearly outlined here. By sharing the loaf, we join that company, which by union with Christ has anticipated entry into the new age, beyond resurrection. The blurring experienced by the harmonized institution narrative is compounded by this further image from St Paul.

Even here, however, we are not left in the hands of Paul for long, for a third extract returns us to the synoptic narratives of Matthew and Luke as we focus on the phrase within the Lord's Prayer, "Give us today our daily bread." We need not dwell in detail on the context, for scholarship is divided and exegesis complex. Suffice to say that many would see clear parallels with this prayer in Jewish literature. This suggests that the phrase in question was not originally symbolic. It referred to daily material needs, or food for the morrow, *epiousios*.[15] The two synoptic texts have different nuances even here. By the time Luke is writing his Gospel, future eschatological considerations are less paramount and it is likely that it is meant to link up with the call to daily renunciation (Luke 9. 23), as being the visible fruits thereof. In the early Christian community it most likely also suggested eucharistic overtones. Now the Lord's Prayer is such an accepted text within liturgy as a whole that it is impossible to be purist about its inclusion, alongside other uses of similar images. Nevertheless, our discussion should have highlighted the further theological variety caused by placing quite different uses of imagery alongside each other. This analysis can be supplemented by looking at some of the optional seasonal material, including sentences which may be included at some point in the rite.

The whole of this exercise builds a picture of a variety of images from different writers, pointing in various directions and certainly not giving a clear focus. It is difficult to understand whether there is underlying intention in such a process of liturgical eclecticism. It even smacks of what might be styled as "concordance theology",[16] that is, scanning the Bible for all references to bread, and pressing all, however mutually incompatible or merely inappropriate, into service. This does not do full justice to the integrity of the biblical writers. The images may be used so as to confuse rather than illuminate. Few people would deny that both Gerard Manley Hopkins and William Wordsworth owed a great deal to nature imagery. Equally, however, few would attempt to press their two very different uses of such imagery into service alongside one another within one text. To attempt such a fusion denies the integrity and creativity of each, and may well mystify the reader rather than lead to poetic clarity.[17]

This is not to deny the continued efficacy of "bread" symbolism. Instead it is to look to a more consistent use of theological/literary sources, and to develop those selected elsewhere in the text so that all may feed upon the richness of the images employed. At the same time, however, this does not presume a protected place for biblical images, nor for the absolute continuity of *any* image. As long as bread remains our staple diet in this culture, it seems difficult to imagine the symbol losing its power. The same may not be true in South-East Asia, where rice is the staple diet, and bread is almost unknown.[18]

We leave our first analysis, however, assuming that this bread symbolism still retains a richness which different eucharistic rites may fail to exploit in its fullness.

—

The whole notion of priesthood continues to undergo theological re-assessment at present. Modern jargon sometimes sees the priest as searching for a role. However priesthood is re-imagined, it is unlikely that sacrificial high priests will again walk the earth in either Christianity or Judaism. Sacrifice as a concept within theology and liturgy has become more nuanced.[19] Has this left us with some moribund imagery? Let us again investigate some passages in the *Common Worship* Eucharist. We can also look to examples in the normative Roman Catholic Paschal Vigil rite.

On this occasion we are less concerned to analyze specific biblical texts, since it is often difficult to discern an exact pedigree for the image. Instead, here are some preliminary reflections upon the biblical material with special reference to "lamb" and "passover" imagery. Within the New Testament, lamb/lamb of God imagery is almost completely Johannine. The two exceptions are in Acts 8. 32 and 1 Peter 1. 18–19. The Acts reference is an Old Testament quotation (Isaiah 53.7–8) used as part of the story of Philip and the Ethiopian eunuch. Any theology derived from the text is very much implicit, as Acts 8. 35 makes clear. The reference in 1 Peter is theologically woven into the text and is used alongside "ransom" language. The entire section of 1 Peter 1. 13–25 is riddled with Old Testament allusions, gathering up references to the "Holiness Code", and later to Isaiah 40. 6–9. Even a veiled reference to the exile, in a typological sense, is there (v. 17). The whole paragraph is designed as a call to the moral life, based upon the ransom effected in the sacrifice of Jesus.

The Johannine use of the imagery is, as we might expect, considerably more subtle. It is introduced early on in John 1. 29, 36, in words from the mouth of John the Baptist. It is one of a list of designations of Jesus, thrown before us in the first chapter, each of which is to play its part in the complex imagery which the evangelist uses to describe the person of

Christic.[20] The intricate weaving of John's tapestry is such that this image is most effectively taken up again in the Passion narrative, when John alters the dating such that Jesus dies at the same time as the slaughtering of the Passover lambs (John 19. 14, 31). Herein lie the sources, then, for much of the liturgical imagery which has made Easter the "Christianized Passover"—the Paschal Feast. The Apocalypse is also, of course, riven with references to the lamb, and it is indeed such references which are often used as planks in the argument which designates Revelation as a product of the Johannine school.

The other chief source of sacrificial imagery in the New Testament is the Epistle to the Hebrews. Here the emphasis is on priesthood, and the irony is that it is the High Priest, Jesus himself, who is sacrificed for us.[21] Both sets of imagery, that of John and of Hebrews, clearly contained heightened dramatic power for a Church growing from Jewish roots. The two theologies are, however, quite different.

Briefly to glance, then, at references in the *Common Worship* eucharistic rite (common to most recent revisions amongst the churches), the first example lies in the *Gloria*: "Lamb of God, you take away the sin of the world." Here we are again back at a revered formula, common to so many rites, and used in a hymn-like manner. The source of the image is clearly John 1. The same image and source can be traced in the *Agnus Dei*: "Jesus, Lamb of God, have mercy on us." The *Agnus Dei* is also a hymn-like formula. Since these are both traditional formulae, we must assume that they will remain within almost all eucharistic rites. As hymns, it is their poetic content and style which is crucial.

The next obvious reference to sacrifice lies in the inherited Cranmerian "comfortable words", translated "he is the propitiation for our sins." The source here is 1 John 2. 2. Whilst the author of the Gospel may not be the same writer as the author of this letter, there is clearly a shared pattern of thought. Perhaps both writers sprang from the same community.[22] The language of propitiatory sacrifice, however, presents its problems and remains theologically contentious.

Moving on to the eucharistic canon in Prayer A, two phrases are significant: "his offering of himself made once for all upon the cross" and "our great high priest". Both these phrases are most obviously traced to the imagery of Hebrews, notably reflecting Hebrews 4. 14 onwards, and then specifically referring in the first phrase to 7. 27, 9. 26–28, and 10. 10 (a similar idea is aired in 1 Peter 3. 18). The same source is the origin of the Easter blessing which is drawn directly from Hebrews 13. 20–21. Here we find ourselves caught up into the language of the Jewish sacrificing high-priesthood. Such language is, of course, highly technical and not immediately comprehensible outside those with an expertise in this area, since such practices ceased more than nineteen hundred years ago. From where does such imagery continue to draw its power? Is there a danger in finding ourselves captive to the tradition?

For further considerations of sacrificial imagery, let us glance at the Roman Catholic Paschal Vigil. There is an intense beauty to this rite; much of this issues from the remarkable use made of light imagery, and the feelings of new creation evoked by the whole atmosphere of Easter. All this, however, is held in an increasing tension as one looks at so much of the symbolism in the rest of the rite. The problem is stated in the title of the rite. It is the Paschal Vigil—the Christian Passover, even to the extent that it takes place in the evening, or at night.

The introduction to the service sets the scene: "This is the passover of the Lord", we are told.[23] Is it perverse to explain the familiar Christian concepts of death and resurrection by means of the less familiar, and again technical, Jewish term "Passover". But we are not left with merely a superficial reference, for in the *Exsultet*, proclaimed by the deacon, we are told, "This is our Passover feast, when Christ, the true Lamb is slain, whose blood consecrates the homes of all believers."[24] How accessible is such imagery to contemporary worshippers? Christ is the equivalent of the Passover Lamb. His blood, like that of the Old Testament sacrificial lamb, is figuratively used to paint the cross upon the door lintel. His blood, then, safeguards the life of those who acknowledge the ransoming power of his blood. Yet the knowledge required for this image to be evocative is at once complex, esoteric, and archaeological in a religious sense. More than that, however, our thanksgiving for deliverance presumably commends, as does the Old Testament narrative, God's annihilation of those outside the covenant, the Egyptians and their contemporary counterparts. Similar *Schadenfreude* seems to present itself with regard to the victims of the other chief image/event remembered in this rite—the Exodus through the Red Sea: an equally archaeological piece of imagery for most Christians.

The Passover image is not left behind, but remains with us throughout the Vigil. Later in the rite, we are reminded of it in prayer: "Father, you teach us in both the Old and the New Testament to celebrate this passover mystery."[25] The image is central, along with the Exodus, to the celebration. Other symbolism is there, notably light, but in terms of narrative and background we remain firmly within the Old Testament.

It was the high priest who sacrificed the lamb and flung its blood against the altar. Indeed, once again, as with bread imagery, different theological strands are harmonized. It is difficult to know when Jesus is the slaughtered lamb of John's Gospel and when he is the self-sacrificing high priest of the Epistle to the Hebrews. There may be a penalty to be paid by mixing such complex imagery. Even separating the strands, however, does not remove the issue. The practices which constitute the non-symbolic origins of the images ceased nearly two thousand years ago.

Images are meant to enlighten and evoke. As Farrer noted, they must begin with our previous experience and take us on. An image is used to catch us up, to integrate and stimulate previously unrelated areas of our experience. To use dead or dying images may be to miss the point of symbolic language. Images certainly must not be banal, nor should they leave us at the point at which we entered. Even so, to begin at a point which is alien to our experience, and requires considerable technical information, empties images of their power. "I feel so desolate," cried the boy's father. "What's desolate?" asked the child. "I can only say I feel like a defeated Spartan after the battle of Thermopylae—that's what desolation is." Doubtless the child went away disappointed in his quest for enlightenment.

The complexity of sacrificial language in the liturgy, and notably in the Eucharist, has been well catalogued elsewhere[26] and no more need be added. Nonetheless, sacrifice remains central to the very message of the Christian gospel. A strand which seems to have run constantly through Christian history has been that often styled "self-giving". It is the pattern offered by St Francis of Assisi and other later saints. Its roots lie firmly within the events surrounding Jesus' life and death. However sceptical the biblical critic, it seems impossible to avoid the suggestion that Jesus taught sacrificial living in this sense. It seems also to be central to Pauline Christianity, "as poor, yet making many rich".[27] But does the type of sacrificial language which we have just analyzed remain the best vehicle with which to convey this truth? Instead, ought we to seek for fresh images to carry across this truth, suitable prisms with which to scatter the colours? In this way, we may sharpen our "feeling after the character of our God", of the possibilities layered then open to us, and finally of our relationship with God.

—

Imagery at its most profound often includes within itself a certain element of impenetrability. There is the excitement of mystery. The total emptiness of the Holy of Holies at the centre of Yahwistic theism exemplifies this at its most effective. The road is frighteningly short, however, between this and an acceptance of inherited obscurity. Our use of Passover imagery forces the point home. It is as if we have absorbed into our thought the Marcan ideal of the parable, the dark saying, the inexplicable riddle or enigma which is there "that they may indeed see but not perceive, and may indeed hear but not understand, lest they should turn again and be forgiven".[28] This may have served Mark's cryptic theological purposes, but it does not easily catch us up into new visions of glory within the liturgy. Images should enlighten us and lead us further forward towards God. Through the prisms should be dispersed ever richer spectral patterns. For this to be so, we must be aware of the pitfalls, but then turn to seek out the clearest glass.

To summarize the problems, then, we can note three areas. They are cultural relativism, the appropriateness of images, and moral concern. We need not dwell long upon the problem of cultural relativity. It is from this source that spring to birth new images and the death of the old. As a phenomenon its importance was canvassed only too thoroughly a generation ago.[29] The second problem is that of the appropriateness of images. Here theology and science have much in common. At one time it seemed helpful for the scientist to liken atoms to billiard-balls. To use earwigs or elephants as models would have been less than appropriate; the analogies would have communicated little. So with theology, the Bible, and liturgy. The deaths of Sisera by tent-peg (Judges 5. 26), or of Ananias and Sapphira (Acts 5. 1ff) as signs and wonders, are not necessarily the best vehicles for communicating God's compassionate love. Furthermore, these examples raise hints of our third problem, that of moral concern. How appropriate is it to use images which celebrate the innocent deaths of many thousands of people, albeit in antiquity? The Passover and the Exodus are undoubtedly two cases in point. The images are there within the canon of Scripture. This, however, gives them no theological immunity. Images may die, become inappropriate, or be seen by later generations as morally indefensible. But ultimately, who is to select, and by what criteria may we select our own preferred images? The Bible clearly demonstrates the wealth of different images, often mutually incompatible, which issue from different people's minds. Each writer could only use those images which spoke to him or her of the things of God. So there are two possible dangers. First is the inappropriate mixing of images. Then, too, there is the danger that Christianity becomes only a past-centred religion, using some images which themselves died two millennia ago. In the case of the Paschal Vigil, some of these images may have died one thousand years earlier still.

The basic message is clear. It is the positive message of needing to take God's present action in the world seriously. So first, the Bible is only one quarry for Christian images. It does not enjoy a uniquely protected position, lying inert to the corrosive influences of critical scholarship and reflection. The second lesson which we may learn is a true grasp of the nature of the poetic imagination and poetic disclosure. Images and their creators must be allowed integrity. Symbolism must be consistently used. Developed images should not be linked uncritically.[30]

The material for developing liturgical imagery lies there richly within our experience. There is no paucity. Indeed, the restricted number of images used relates to our lack of imagination and adventure. This is true of our use of the Bible, the tradition of the Christian past beginning with the Fathers, and the creative possibilities of the present day. So, in looking to the *Easter* Vigil (note the change of terms), the Bible is packed with apposite images, be it Ezekiel's new heart (Ezekiel 36. 26), Jeremiah's new covenant (Jeremiah 31. 31), or Paul's new creation (2 Corinthians 5. 17). Often to use such images will require what Farrer termed rebirth—they arise phoenix-like from the ashes with a new guise, but filled with a new power.

Yet human experience calls forth so many more images. Paul Tillich, whose theology has undergone something of an eclipse in many areas, was nevertheless masterful in his art of the multiplication of images. His use of the Bible need not be laboured; whilst unorthodox it was still a strong component of his thought. One of his key theological themes, the "Ground of our Being", he quarried from the treasury of Augustine. Then, elsewhere, he would coin quite new concepts, using insights from literature, human experience, and the human sciences. Ultimate concern, alienation, and ontological shock are just three of the better known examples.[31] Much of Tillich's language has a slightly studied academic feel to it, but his sermons showed the master at work in the liturgical situation.[32] How, then, may new images be developed, that is, new images in worship, centred upon the themes of Christian love, self-giving, and our relationship with God?

Christianity's survival depends upon its relationship to the daily life of the human community. Such life springs partly from the irreducible place of imagery in theistic discourse. Christianity is a hardy plant which has weathered many winters. Throughout its life it has been frequently pruned but has constantly thrown out new shoots. Still, we must not starve its growth, allow its leaves to turn yellow, or make it barren of fruit. The sources of food, as with any healthy plant, are many and various. For Christian liturgy, images are there in plenty. They are found in the richness of poetic religious discourse, coming down through the ages and still pouring forth. Let not growth be stunted by a dearth of imaginative gardeners.

NOTES

1. First published as "The Bible, Symbolism and Liturgy" in *Symbolism and the Liturgy II* (Grove Liturgical Study 26, 1981); reproduced here by kind permission of Grove Books Ltd. (<https://www.grovebooks.co.uk>). Hugh Montefiore in *Thinking about the Eucharist: Papers by Members of the Church of England Doctrine Commission* (SCM, 1972), p. 70. Hugh Montefiore talked of a specific form of reflection involved in liturgy, for which he coined the term "worship thinking".

2. Edwyn Bevan, *Symbolism and Belief* (Allen and Unwin, 1938), pp. 11–14.

3. Austin Farrer, *The Glass of Vision* (Bampton Lectures 1948; Dacre Press, 1949), pp. 86–92; see also Farrer, *A Rebirth of Images: the making of St John's Apocalypse* (Dacre Press, 1949), and cf. a similar view seen in the Welsh priest/poet R. S. Thomas: " . . . in any case, poetry is religion, religion is poetry. The message of the New Testament is poetry. Christ was a poet, the New Testament is a metaphor, the Resurrection is a metaphor; and I feel perfectly within my rights in approaching my whole vocation as priest and as preacher as one who is to present poetry; and when I preach poetry I am preaching Christianity, and when one discusses Christianity one is discussing poetry in its imaginative aspects." It would seem that this quotation came originally from a television programme, but I have culled it from the journal *Poetry Wales* Vol. 14 No. 4 (Spring 1979), p. 11.

4. Farrer, *The Glass of Vision*, p. 74.

5. Artur Weiser, *The Psalms: A Commentary*, trans. Herbert Hartwell (SCM, 1962); Ivan Engnell, *Critical Essays on the Old Testament*, trans. John T. Willis (SPCK, 1970), pp. 68ff.; Sigmund Mowinckel, *The Psalms in Israel's Worship*, trans. D. R. Ap-Thomas (Blackwell, 1963, 2 Volumes).

6. Farrer, *The Glass of Vision*, p. 125. Emphasis added.

7. Ibid., p. 135.

8. Ibid., p. 119.

9. Christopher Evans makes this point in "The Eucharist and Symbolism in the New Testament", in *Thinking about the Eucharist*, pp. 60ff. He compares it to the Passover in this sense.

10. Eucharistic Prayers A, B, & C. Prayer C is a direct descendant of Cranmer's rite and especially as revised in the deposited 1928 *Book of Common Prayer*.

11. For a good summary see H. B. Green, *The Gospel according to Matthew* (OUP, 1975), pp. 212ff.

12. See, for example, C. K. Barrett, *A Commentary on the First Epistle to the Corinthians* (Black, 1968), pp. 266–7. He notes that it is recounting the deliverance afforded by Christ in his death, and represented in the supper (one should also note that if the Gospel passion narratives were liturgical in origin, then each version has its own integrity in worship).

13. Ibid., p. 233.

14. See the picture as given in the story of the stilling of the storm (Matthew 8. 23–27) and especially the treatment of G. Bornkamm, G. Barth, and H. J. Held, *Tradition and Interpretation in Matthew* (SCM, 1963), pp. 52–57 and *ad loc.*

15. Green, *The Gospel according to Matthew*, p. 90, and E. Franklin, *Christ the Lord* (SPCK, 1975), p. 151 (Bible. refs. Matthew 6. 11, Luke 11. 3).

16. I am grateful to Miss Elizabeth Moore for this label!

17. As an exercise in demonstrating this, I would suggest a sensitive reading of Wordsworth's "Ode on Intimations of Immortality" alongside Hopkins' "The Windhover" and "God's Grandeur". Not only do they derive different points from the images used, but also their use of imagery in terms of style is quite different.

18. This point is made forcibly by M. F. Wiles in "Grace in Church and Sacrament", in *Theology* Vol. 72 (October 1969), p. 458. He writes, "Was the historic fact of the last supper that Christ took bread and wine and transformed them to a newer and deeper use or was it rather a question of his taking for his purpose the staple foods of his place and time?" This, of course, raises the thorny question of how important it is to re-enact the historical details of the rite as we have them, or how much more important is the principle behind it, if we could be sure we knew what that was. Wiles makes a similar point about the practicalities of baptism by total immersion in the cold rivers of North-West Europe.

19. Note my own chapter on sacrifice in this volume, Chapter 5.

20. Other designations include "Son of God" (John 1. 34, 49), "Rabbi" (John 1. 38, 49), "the Messiah" (John 1. 41), "him of whom Moses in the law and also the prophets wrote" (John 1. 45), "king of Israel" (John 1. 47).

21. See J. Hering, *The Epistle to the Hebrews* (Epworth, 1970), p. 64.

22. See J. L. Houlden, *A Commentary on the Johannine Epistles* (Black, 1973).

23. *Sunday Missal* (Collins Text, 1975), Paschal Vigil, p. 208.

24. Paschal Vigil, p. 211.

25. Paschal Vigil, p. 228.

26. J. L. Houlden in *Thinking about the Eucharist*, pp. 81ff.

27. See 2 Corinthians 6. 10 and Philippians 2. 5–11 (even if this is a quotation from a pre-Pauline hymn, he clearly quotes it in an affirmative manner), for just two examples in Paul.

28. Mark 4. 11–12 (RSV).

29. See D. E. Nineham, *The Use and Abuse of the Bible* (MacMillan, 1976); and, for a critique, J. Barton, "Reflections on Cultural Relativism", in *Theology* Vol. 82 (March 1979), p. 103; as *Theology* (May 1979), p. 191.

30. The longer Post-Communion prayer in the Rite A Eucharist includes some very sensitive use of images, but fails before the final tribunal due to their mixing. At different moments, God "is meeting us in his Son", "bringing us home", "giving grace", and "opening the gate", whilst we are giving "light to the world" and being kept "firm in the hope" etc.

31. For all this, see Paul Tillich, *Systematic Theology,* Vols. I-III (Combined Volume, James Nisbet, 1968), but also his sermons; note his use of "new creation, covenant, heart, Jerusalem" imagery, for example, in "Behold, I am Doing a New Thing" in Tillich, *The Shaking of the Foundations* (Penguin, 1962), pp. 174ff.

32. Tillich, *The Shaking of the Foundations, ad loc.* See also the various collections of Austin Farrer's sermons for a supreme example of how to use imagery; e.g. Austin Farrer, *The Essential Sermons,* selected and edited by Leslie Houlden (SPCK, 1991).

7.   LITURGICAL LIVING: LEARNING BY MIMESIS[1]

There was nothing short of a revolution in liturgical study in the final quarter of the twentieth century. It was a revolution which built upon the successes of the Liturgical Movement. That movement, which traces its origins much further back, perhaps to the latter part of the nineteenth century, rekindled an interest in and focus upon the historical study of liturgy. It is not necessary to rehearse the unfolding of this renaissance, nor to tabulate the names of the *dramatis personae* through whom the movement was conceived and achieved, but suffice to say that this renewal of historical theology within liturgical study was perhaps the key to liturgical reform in all traditions. The great flowering of liturgical reform through the Second Vatican Council and across the Reformed and Anglican traditions was rooted initially in historical analysis of the early patterns of worship. This meant that up until two generations ago, much study both in universities and seminaries was largely historically focused and textually based. The literature of the period testifies to this. Joseph Jungmann's *Mass of the Roman Rite* was the classic of the genre.[2] Within the Church of England a similar pre-occupation predominated. Alongside study of the patristic material, much time was given to an analysis of the development of the 1662 *Book of Common Prayer* during the Henrician, Edwardian, and Elizabethan periods of the sixteenth century: Geoffrey Cuming's work reflects these emphases.[3]

Nonetheless, it is important in understanding the more recent revolution to acknowledge the particular contribution of some others who broadened the scope of liturgical study. One notable source here was the work pioneered at the Benedictine monastery at Maria Laach in the Rheinland. Odo Casel's seminal work on the *mystery* which is at the heart of the liturgy recounted the importance of the regular rehearsing of the drama of salvation, and so of the performative nature of Christian liturgy: it is the story which stands central.[4] Alongside this stand other pioneering writings. Father Gabriel Hebert SSM explored the historical background and sources, but also offered a broader interpretation from an Anglican perspective. Hebert again shifted the focus to a performative approach where worship effectively defined the nature of the Church.[5] At the same time as this, there was a growing interest in liturgy, symbolism, and phenomenology. The Romanian theologian Mircea Eliade linked his approach with the work of Carl Gustav Jung.[6] He reflected upon the significance of the imagination and the unconscious in relation to religious structures, and so liturgical worship. This development, which constitutes the revolution in liturgical study in the latter part of the twentieth century, took the historical approach and integrated it into a broader, performative, phenomenologically rooted liturgical theology. This focused not so much on what worship *is* but instead upon what worship *does* in the present, that is, how it operates and how, through the liturgy, God works out his purposes for us and the world. This has revolutionized both the teaching of liturgy and also more recent liturgical revision: even the titles of more recent monographs and reflections upon Christian worship have mirrored this revolution.[7]

—

What, then, might this revolution mean for the liturgy itself and, remembering the work of both Hebert and Casel, what impact will it have both on our understanding of the nature of the Church and our formation into Christ? In attempting to see a little more deeply into that question let us revert briefly to a period when such a revolution had not yet taken hold, a time, indeed, not far distant from the writing of Gabriel Hebert's *Liturgy and Society*. The following account was published in 1935 but was probably describing life just five or ten years earlier. We are in the village of Hetton, probably in Bedfordshire. The vicar is about to ascend the pulpit for the Christmas sermon:

The vicar . . . was an elderly man who had served in India most of his life. [The patron's] father had given him the living at the instance of his dentist. His sermons had been composed in his more active days for delivery at the garrison chapel; he had done nothing to adapt them to the changed conditions of his ministry and they mostly concluded with some reference to homes and dear ones far away. The villagers did not find this in any way surprising. Few of the things said in church seemed to have any particular reference to themselves. "How difficult it is for us," he began, blandly surveying his congregation, who coughed into their mufflers and chafed their chilblains under their woollen gloves, "to realise that this is indeed Christmas. Instead of glowing log fire and windows tight shuttered against the drifting snow, we have only the harsh glare of an alien sun; instead of the happy circle of loved faces, of home and family, we have the uncomprehending stares of the subjugated, though no doubt grateful, heathen. Instead of the placid ox and ass of Bethlehem," said the vicar, slightly losing the thread of his comparisons, "we have for companions the ravening tiger and the exotic camel, the furtive jackal and the ponderous elephant."[8]

Evelyn Waugh was never known, of course, for his reserve in irony or in drawing caricatures taken from life. Nevertheless, despite the overdrawn portrait, there are enough elements of truth to drive the point home. *Performance* of the liturgy alone cannot be relied upon to communicate the faith. This is true not only when it includes the homiletic technique of the sort manifested by "the Revd Tendril", as Waugh calls him in that brief cameo, but also in the more general performance of the liturgy as a whole. Indeed, liturgical performance can obfuscate as much as it can reveal unless the act of worship is seen to be part of a continued initiation into the life of faith. Liturgy needs to be performed *well* and clearly focused—first and primarily upon God but then also on the formation of the Church, the people of God.

Even so, the notion that the liturgy is the primary and—for many Christians—the only regular source of learning and teaching of the faith goes back to the roots of the tradition, and beyond that to the soil of the Hebrew scriptures out of which much of our tradition sprang. At the heart of this lies the pattern of "mimesis", a term used by both Plato and Aristotle. For both of them mimesis was the imitation and perfection of nature. Plato and Aristotle both use the term, in particular, in relation to poetry and art, even though they differ in their interpretation. Aristotle notes, "For the medium being the same, and the objects the same, the poet may imitate by narration—in which case he can either take another personality as Homer does, or speak in his own person, unchanged—or he may present all his characters as living and moving before us."[9]

Within the Christian tradition, however, that pattern of mimesis can be used more widely to capture the way in which truth is communicated and performatively fashions character. This usage was developed classically by Erich Auerbach in his literary critical essay which he titled simply, *Mimesis*. For Auerbach mimesis is crucial for understanding the nature of both Old and New Testament literature. The key issue is not one of "crude history" but rather the performative living out of truth. So, talking of the biblical narratives, he writes that:

> ... the moral, religious and psychological phenomena which are their sole concern are made concrete in the sensible matter of life.[10]

Later he writes, for example, of Mark's Gospel:

> Without any effort on [St Mark's] part, as it were, and purely through the inner movement of what he relates, the story becomes visually concrete. And the story speaks to everybody; everybody is urged and indeed required to take sides for or against it. Even ignoring it implies taking sides.[11]

The story, then, becomes inalienably associated with those who hear it. This is part of what Auerbach calls the "figural imagination". He comments:

> "Figural imagination" establishes a connection between two
> events or persons in such a way that the first signifies not
> only itself but also the second, while the second involves
> or fulfils the first. The two poles of a figure are separated
> in time, but both, being real events or persons, are within
> temporality. They are contained in the flowing stream which
> is historical life, and only the comprehension, the *intellectus
> spiritualis*, of their interdependence is a spiritual act.[12]

This discovery is crucial. It defines the nature of an image, using two
apparently unlike people, events, or objects together in a new way which
thereby communicates truth. This is the moment in which the spiritual/
divine truth is made visible. It is an argument similar to that used by
Austin Farrer in his Bampton Lectures. Farrer's concern is to explore
how scripture communicates divine truth. Prescinding from a purely
propositional view of revelation with all its attendant difficulties, Farrer,
in an innovative manner, indicates how Christian truth is purveyed
through a series of controlling images which surface in the different
genres of literature in the books of the Old and New Testaments. In an
illuminating passage, Farrer argues:

> I would no longer attempt with the psalmist, "to set God
> before my face". I would see him as the underlying cause of
> my thinking, especially in those thoughts in which I tried
> to think of him. I would dare to hope that sometimes my
> thought would become diaphanous, so that there should
> be some perception of the divine cause shining through the
> created effect, as a deep pool, settling into a clear tranquillity,
> permits us to see the spring in the bottom of it from which
> its waters rise. I would dare to hope that through a second
> cause the First Cause might be felt, when the second cause in
> question was itself a spirit, made in the image of the divine
> Spirit, and perpetually welling up out of his creative act.[13]

The Aristotelian roots of Farrer's thought here are clearly visible but, as
with Aristotle, the logic is rooted in the earth of the empirically human.

Farrer argues his case using prophecy, alongside narrative from scripture and necessarily also wisdom, remembering his roots in philosophy and reason. It is this approach which underpins much of his biblical scholarship, prefiguring some of the literary critical approaches to scripture which thrive alongside some more recent narrative approaches to Christian theology. Farrer arrives at a key conjunction between narrative, poetry, and prose, and the communication of divine truth. Farrer's genius was to bring together natural and revealed theology in a manner which saw the figural imagination as seminal; herein lie too the seeds of a liturgical and theological mimesis. This conjunction is a key realisation for us in regard to the liturgy and theological cognition. As we find ourselves addressed by the biblical text so, in a similar manner, we are engaged by the liturgy so that the story of our own individual life and our common life together become part of the history of salvation. Neither pole is unaffected by that conjunction. Indeed, both our life and the story of salvation are *renewed* and *transformed* by this relationship.

—

If the biblical material is not only *used* in the liturgy, but often itself originated from or for the liturgy, then this pattern of mimesis stands at the heart of what we are about. We learn and are formed "performatively" by the liturgy and this is a truth which is manifest throughout Christian history. It is there in the daily and weekly celebration of the Eucharist, but it is there too in the catechetical tradition again reaching back to the patristic period. Edward Yarnold, writing on the mystagogical catecheses, captured this well.[14] He wrote in the preface to his book about that tradition:

> Everything was calculated to inspire religious awe, to make these rites the occasion of a profound and life-long conversion.[15]

The key here is that Christian formation comes about through liturgical rites, and indeed it is the mystery—or mystagogy as it became known—that was integral to the process of teaching and learning. So Yarnold notes:

The ceremonies took place at night, some of them in the
dark, after weeks of intense preparation; they were wrapped
in secrecy, and the candidate knew little about them until
just before, or even after, he had received them.[16]

Here, then, we encounter again this same process of *mimesis*, of entering
into the narrative of salvation. The patristic sermons which form the
heart of this liturgical/catechetical process are quite clear about this
themselves. So Theodore of Mopsuestia writes of the true end of the
catechetical process:

With this end in view we have obtained by God's grace the
favour of celebrating this mystery now, and of enjoying
the kingdom of heaven and all the indescribable blessings
which will last for ever and which we shall all receive by
the grace of our Lord Jesus Christ.[17]

This is a tradition which has been recaptured and which owes its inheritance
not only to the mystagogical catecheses of the early Church, but also to
the Jewish roots of Christianity with the telling of the history of salvation
in the *seder* meal. This recaptured tradition is clear in contemporary
processional and stational rites. It is clear in the use of movement in
baptism and confirmation. The liturgical space is used as the locus of a
journey which takes this history of salvation and encourages both the
individual baptizand and also the worshipping community once again
to combine *the* story with *their* story. It is supremely clear in the Paschal
Vigil where the *Exsultet* sets out the pattern of salvation. It does so by
the dramatic mimetic process of repeatedly declaring that, "This is the
night" (when heaven descended to earth, and so on). The juxtaposition
of the *historical* night and the night in which the worshippers stand
means that the liturgical caucus makes that salvation its own through a
pilgrimage or journey within the liturgy. Presumably this also explains the
continued popularity of oratorios like Handel's *Messiah* at Christmas or
Bach's settings of the Passions at Easter. Such texts do not become worn
by repetition, but instead, "re-inhabited" by rehearsal, owned by those
who perform them through mimesis.

This pattern establishes too the tradition of liturgical and catechetical formation renewed in the Roman Catholic RCIA, the Rite of Christian Initiation of Adults. It is a tradition that has been embraced by a number of churches through the twentieth-century catechetical movement, but it stands as such within a still wider sweep of tradition. The monastic life also sees the liturgy as a seminal, if not *the* seminal, means by which we are made into the image of Christ. The daily recitation of the hours is once again a form of mimesis. Not only the hours of daylight, but the entire corpus of time is interwoven with prayer which recites the drama of both incarnation and redemption. The survival of the night-stair at Hexham Abbey and elsewhere reminds us of the continual formation into the likeness of Christ which is the monastic way throughout both day and night. St Benedict memorably captures this in the Prologue to his rule:

> We propose, therefore, to establish a school of the Lord's service, and in setting it up we hope we shall lay down nothing that is harsh or hard to bear.[18]

Then also, in the Epilogue, he writes:

> Whoever you are, then, who are hurrying forward to your heavenly fatherland, do you with Christ's help fulfil this little Rule written for beginners; and then you will come at the end, under God's protection, to those heights of learning and virtue which we have mentioned above.[19]

Of course, both of these reflections relate to the entire Rule, but at the heart of this Rule is the *opus Dei* and the life of prayer—*orare est laborare, laborare est orare*. That is, the essence of the "hours" was the interweaving of all things, day and night, by inhabiting a liturgical rhythm. Both here in the monastic life and, indeed, more generally in the life of the Church, it is the process of repetition and regularity which helps habituate both the individual and the community into virtue. This is part of the work of mimesis: it helps root the "habits of the heart", to use Alexis de Tocqueville's coinage.[20] The recent recovery of the Aristotelian moral-philosophical tradition with its rooting in character, and thus the subsequent formation of character, is resonant with this. Alasdair MacIntyre's rediscovery of the essential role of virtue was seminal in seeing the continuity of the Aristotelian moral tradition within Western thought. In this he has sown seeds which have grown prolifically.[21] This emphasis on character has been most energetically pursued, amongst Christian theologians, by Stanley Hauerwas. Hauerwas, once again, is keen to stress the formative nature of the Christian liturgy. Character is formed both within the individual and the community through prayer and worship. His is a mimetic approach in all but name.[22]

———

This pattern of prayerful habituation stands, too, at the centre of the Anglican tradition. Part of the genius of Cranmer was to take the monastic hours of prayer and, with remarkable imagination and sensitivity, to gather them into two daily offices which would frame and thus form the life of every Christian. The aim and intention of Morning and Evening Prayer was to fashion a pattern of liturgical prayer which would be accessible and a realistic pattern for all who would form their lives after the likeness of Christ. Such a pattern of prayer remains both essential for and required of all Church of England clergy.

Cranmer's inheritance, developed to some degree in the 1559 Prayer Book and then again in 1662, is one which aims to offer a renewed pattern of mimesis through which the Christian soul is offered to God. It is there not only in the offices themselves, but in the Coverdale Psalter, ordered to be said morning and evening within each month. It is there too in the pastoral offices and in the rites of initiation; a basic framework for catechesis is at the heart of Cranmer's catechism. The classical formula used by the bishops in the rite of confirmation reminds all Christians that discipleship is something which follows each one of us throughout our lives; the prayer is almost a prototype for the now rather overused image of the Christian life as a journey:

> Defend, O Lord, this thy Servant with thy heavenly grace,
> that he may continue thine forever; and daily increase in

thy Holy Spirit, more and more, until he come unto thy
everlasting kingdom.

The mimetic pattern is a lifelong discipline and pattern into which each
Christian soul is inducted in baptism and confirmation.

The rubrics preceding the order for Holy Communion make clear the
formative nature of the liturgy, as indeed does the pattern of prayer itself.
Often criticized for its "over-penitential" mood, nonetheless the emphasis
on true penitence and preparation makes clear the formational nature of
the rite. In a resonant phrase, this intention is gathered up perfectly in
the prayer of thanksgiving after communion:

> And we most humbly beseech thee, O heavenly Father, so
> to assist us with thy grace, that we may continue in that
> holy fellowship, and do all such good works as thou hast
> prepared for us to walk in.

Placing Cranmer's pattern of prayer alongside the fact that the Church of
England has no declaratory confessional documents points in a focused
manner to Anglicanism being rooted in the tradition of *lex orandi, lex
credendi*. This is illustrated well in the preface to the "Declaration of
Assent" used at all institutions, ordinations, and similar rites:

> The Church of England is part of the One, Holy, Catholic
> and Apostolic Church, worshipping the one true God,
> Father, Son, and Holy Spirit. It professes the faith uniquely
> revealed in the Holy Scriptures and set forth in the catholic
> creeds, which faith the Church is called upon to proclaim
> afresh in each generation. Led by the Holy Spirit, it has
> borne witness to Christian truth in its historic formularies,
> the Thirty-nine Articles of Religion, the [1662] Book of
> Common Prayer, and the Ordering of Bishops, Priests,
> and Deacons. In the declaration you are about to make,
> will you affirm your loyalty to this inheritance of faith as
> your inspiration and guidance under God in bringing the

grace and truth of Christ to this generation and making
Him known to those in your care?

The 1662 *Book of Common Prayer*, along with the other "historic
formularies", has a seminal role within the Church of England's life and
polity. Cranmer, then, took over in his own way that same pattern and
tradition of mimesis which can be traced back to the biblical witness
and to the patristic period. Mimesis means the rehearsal of a tradition
performatively such that the key defining images of the Christian faith
help fashion the lives of believers. This same mimetic tradition does
indeed lie as the foundation for the recent initiative of the Church of
England, *Transforming Worship*. The initiative seeks to rediscover a pattern
which can help to form the people of God, individually and corporately,
through the daily and weekly rehearsing of the liturgy in all its forms
and manifestations.[23]

It would narrow the discussion unnecessarily and inappropriately to
leave this argument purely within the context of the Church of England
or Anglican polity and piety. The roots of the Church of England lie
in the controversies and wider context of the Reformation in Europe.
That seismic movement, however, both erupted out of and continued
to nurture a strand that goes deep into the sub-structure of Christian
life, liturgy, and theology. It is that strand which we know as "Christian
Humanism". Erasmus of Rotterdam (who remained loyal to the Bishop
of Rome) was a noted humanist and a key figure behind the development
of the Reformation.

—

Nonetheless, that pattern of life and thought which became known as
humanism remains a continuing part of the essential sub-structure
of Christian tradition. Most often it is traced back to the sixteenth-
century Renaissance. Placed within Renaissance thought it points back,
of course, towards the very foundations of Christian faith and culture,
notably in the Byzantine Empire. The roots of Christian humanism run
deep and are rooted in the liturgy. The pattern of *lex orandi, lex credendi*
runs through Orthodox thought. So, for example, when Anglicans were

recently seeking out the basis of an Orthodox comment on Mary in the tradition of Christian thought, within a wider dialogue with Roman Catholics, the Orthodox theologian consulted quoted neither a creed nor the declarations of the early Councils. Instead, her quotation came from a seventh-century antiphon: both Christian doctrine and life then spring from the liturgy. The apostle Paul himself writes of the need for us to be formed into the likeness of Christ; our very way of life is a living sacrifice and a spiritual worship. Mimesis has deep Christian roots. In his recent spirited, profound, and sometimes polemical apologium for the revolutionary nature of Christendom and the Christian tradition, David Bentley Hart writes:

> It might be better, therefore, simply to note that what it is for us to be human—what, that is, our aesthetic and moral imagination are capable of—is determined by the encompassing narrative of reality we inhabit. First, for any people, comes its story, and then whatever is possible for that people becomes conceivable within that story. For centuries the Christian story shaped and suffused our civilisation.[24]

This sets Christian life and liturgy within the widest context imaginable. It is the Christian story which "shaped and suffused" Western civilization. That story has been lived for two millennia by an unimaginably various and kaleidoscopic host of individuals and communities who have themselves been shaped by the same narrative, the same mystery. Much of that which is richest in Western civilization is a product or even a facet of that view of humanity which is suffused by divinity as seen in the person of Jesus Christ. The Eastern tradition talks of theosis or divinization. Through a process of perichoresis we are caught up into the divine energies and transformed by God's power; God became human that we might partake in the divine. This theosis is a direct product or fruit of mimesis, of performing, being part of a liturgy which rehearses the *mysterious* narrative into which we are born, or formed into, every day of our lives. That narrative is shaped by the mystery of the life, passion, death, and resurrection of Jesus Christ. Liturgical living is learning by mimesis to be part of that mystery. The "glory of a living human being", the triumph of the Christian humanistic spirit, are the fruits of mimesis. In the liturgical revolution of the last two generations we have begun to relearn whence these fruits come.

NOTES

1. An earlier, shorter version of this article was presented to the *Returning to the Church* conference at St Stephen's House in 2010. First published as "Liturgical Living: Learning by Mimesis", in *Anaphora* Vol. 5 No. 1 (June 2011), pp. 23–38, ISSN 1755–9790; reproduced here by kind permission of the editors.

2. Joseph A. Jungmann, *The Mass of the Roman Rite* (Burnes and Oates, 1959).

3. Geoffrey Cuming, *A History of Anglican Liturgy* (Macmillan, 1969).

4. George Guiver CR, *Pursuing the Mystery: Worship and Daily Life as Presences of God* (SPCK, 1996) and Odo Casel, ed. Burkhard Neunheuser, *The Mystery of Christian Worship and Other Writings* (Newman Press and Darton, Longman and Todd, 1962).

5. A. G. Hebert SSM, *Liturgy and Society: The Function of the Church in the Modern World* (Faber, 1935).

6. Mircea Eliade, trans. W. R. Trask, *The Myth of the Eternal Return, Or, Cosmos and History* (Princeton University Press, 1954).

7. Christopher Irvine, *The Art of God: The Making of Christians and the Meaning of Worship* (SPCK, 2005) and David Stancliffe, *God's Pattern: Shaping our Worship, Ministry and Life* (SPCK, 2003).

8. Evelyn Waugh, *A Handful of Dust* (Chapman and Hall, 1934), p. 32.

9. From Aristotle's *Poetics*.

10. Erich Auerbach, trans. Willard Trask, *Mimesis: The Representation of Reality in Western Literature* (Princeton University Press, 1953), p. 14.

11. Ibid., p. 48.

12. Ibid., p. 73.

13. Austin Farrer, *The Glass of Vision* (Bampton Lectures 1948; Dacre Press, 1949), p. 8.

14. Edward Yarnold SJ, *The Awe-Inspiring Rites of Initiation: the Origins of the R.I.C.A.* (T & T Clark, 1971).

15. Ibid., p. ix.

16. Ibid., p. ix

17. Ibid., p. 250.

18. David Parry OSB (trans.), *The Rule of St Benedict* (Darton, Longman and Todd, 1980), p. 4.

19. Ibid., p. 197.

20. Stephen Platten, "The Uses of Liturgy: Worship Nourishing Mission", in *Worship* Vol. 83 No. 3 (2009), pp. 234–249; reprinted in Chapter 9 of this book.

21. Robert Bellah et al., *Habits of the Heart: Individualism and Commitment in American Life* (University of California Press, 1996).

22. Stanley Hauerwas, *A Community of Character: Toward a Constructive Christian Social Ethic* (University of Notre Dame Press, 1981).

23. A Report of the Church of England's Liturgical Commission, *Transforming Worship: Living the New Creation* (GS1651, 2007). Available online (<https://churchofengland.org/media/1251048/gs1651.pdf>).

24. David Bentley Hart, *Atheist Delusions: The Christian Revolution and its Fashionable Enemies* (Yale University Press, 2009), p. 239.

8. ALL SUCH GOOD WORKS: THE BOOK OF COMMON PRAYER AND THE FASHIONING OF ENGLISH SOCIETY[1]

"And we most humbly beseech thee, O heavenly Father, so to assist us with thy grace, that we may continue in that holy fellowship, and do all such good works as thou hast prepared for us to walk in; through Jesus Christ our Lord, to whom, with thee and the Holy Ghost, be all honour and glory, world without end. Amen."

So concludes the second of the two post-communion prayers in the 1662 "Order for the Administration of the Lord's Supper or Holy Communion". That prayer, generally referred to as the "Prayer of Thanksgiving", is a finely balanced piece of theological prose. There is no doubt as to the desired effectiveness of the rite: "we . . . [should] . . . do all such good works as thou hast prepared for us to walk in." It is an *improving* rite and the intention is that piety and devotion should have an immediate impact upon our behaviour, and it is *our* behaviour; it is not a purely individual matter. Worship is a corporate act and so it is *we* who should "continue in that holy fellowship, and do all such good works as thou hast prepared for *us* to walk in." So one of the most powerful effects of Cranmer's translation of the liturgy into the vernacular was to overcome the danger of the communion rite becoming largely an individual act of piety, relating each person to their Creator and Redeemer.[2]

Another element in the balance of this passage and of the rite as a whole is the rooting of all in grace. This was not simply an outflow of the

Lutheran emphasis on "justification by faith alone" with its subsequent rejection of salvation by works. It also stood in continuity with western catholic mainstream teaching on grace. Through this understanding, the liturgy remains the *opus Dei*. It is primarily God's act into which we are incorporated through grace. Both the Christian community (the Church) and individual members of the faithful are fashioned by God through worship. The significance of this prevenient grace is easily lost. Even in contemporary liturgical revision, this lesson has not always been learned. So, for example, the contemporary form of the Collect for Advent begins:

> Almighty God, give us grace to cast away the works of
> darkness and to put on the armour of light, now in the
> time of this mortal life . . .

This is a significant shift from Cranmer's version, followed in the 1662 *Book of Common Prayer*, which reads:

> Almighty God, give us grace that we may cast away the
> works of darkness, and put upon us the armour of light,
> now in the time of this mortal life . . .

In the original version, the initiative remains firmly in the hands of God. God's grace makes it possible for us to cast away the works of darkness and *God* "puts upon us" the armour of light. We are created by God and further fashioned through our participation in the liturgy, which is itself the o*pus Dei*. This remains a crucial realization, especially as one explores how the liturgy is transformative,[3] and it also lies at the heart of the impact of the *Book of Common Prayer* upon Church and society, in its varied revisions between 1549 and 1662.

   Cranmer begins with the formative and transformative aims of the Prayer Book in his Preface to the 1549 edition, which is later incorporated into the 1662 book, with minor revisions, as "Concerning the Service of the Church". Cranmer praises the tradition of "common prayers" in the Church, and notes how they have been corrupted. He continues with reference to common prayer:

The first original and ground whereof, if a man would search out by the ancient Fathers, he shall find, that the same was not ordained but of a good purpose, and for a great advancement of godliness: For they so ordered the matter, that all the whole Bible (or the greatest part thereof) should be read over once every year; intending thereby, that the Clergy, and especially such as were Ministers in the congregation, should (by often reading, and meditation in God's word) be stirred up to godliness themselves, and be more able also to exhort others by wholesome doctrine, and to confute them that were adversaries to the truth; and further, that the people (by daily hearing of holy Scripture read in the Church) might continually profit more and more in the knowledge of God, and be the more inflamed with the love of his true Religion.[4]

Holy Scripture is at the heart of this preface, but it is clear that the whole enterprise of the new *Book of Common Prayer* is to bring liturgy and worship to the people, both in the vernacular and in a manner which is accessible to all. Godliness of the people is its aim and ultimately such godliness is achievable by God and God alone. Later on, Cranmer notes:

So that here you have an Order for Prayer (as touching the reading of holy Scripture) much agreeable to the mind and purpose of the old Fathers, and a great deal more profitable and commodious, than that which of late was used.

Later still, we read:

It is also more commodious, both for the shortness thereof, and for the plainness of the Order, and for the Rules that be few and easy. Furthermore by this order, the curates shall need none other books for their public service, but this book and the Bible: by the means whereof, the people shall not be at so great charge for books, as in time past they have been.

All that we have noted so far is further endorsed in the exhortations within the Holy Communion rite. In the 1662 Prayer Book, the first exhortation gives notice that the priest is to administer the sacrament and that those who wish to partake of the sacrament should duly prepare themselves, examining their lives and if he or she:

> requireth further comfort . . . he may receive the benefit of absolution, together with ghostly counsel and advice, to the quieting of his conscience, and avoiding of all scruple and doubtfulness.

The second exhortation once again reminds the prospective communicant of God's initiative in worship. Again the worshipper is called to reflection:

> These things if ye earnestly consider, ye will by God's grace return to a better mind.

Then finally, in the third exhortation, the spiritual nourishment received from the sacrament is affirmed:

> For as the benefit is great, if with a true penitent heart and lively faith we receive that holy Sacrament . . .

Although the linguistic expression may now feel both archaic and even arcane, the profound understanding of the nature of worship is unquestionable. Cranmer, and those who followed him in the revisions of the 1559, 1604, and 1662 Prayer Books, understood that worship lay at the heart of human flourishing and fulfilment. Worship was not only for the priestly caste (the "curates"), nor indeed purely as devotional work for the individual. It was neither a pastime for the sophisticated alone nor an interesting addition to life for those who desired it. Instead, worship and ritual lay at the heart of a healthy society. This was the perception of Thomas Cranmer and his liturgical successors. It is an understanding which has been pushed too easily to the margins of the life of the Church, the individual, and the community.

Ritual, then, is a key element within the corporate life of nations, and notably religious rites. In a reflection on the crucial significance of worship, Michael Stancliffe traces this essential aspect of our humanity back to primitive societies. He notes:

> . . . primitive man has a much simpler, more direct, basic and elemental motive in performing his rites than keeping or getting on the right side of God.[5]

He continues:

> In other words, his aim—indeed his overriding pre-occupation—is to make contact, as frequently and continuously as possible, with that unchanging reality upon which his and all life depends and so to ensure that, despite all the flux of change or decay, life in his visible world is constantly renewed and enhanced. This he does by performing certain rituals; he practices religion; he worships.[6]

Worship, then, relates to an innate human need which nourishes and edifies a healthy community. It is partly expressed within us as individuals, but it is essential to the health of any community. Stancliffe later writes:

> So it is for the renewal and re-inforcement of their society, not of their individual selves, that primitive men perform their rituals. Their worship has a public not a private reference. Indeed a primitive society is largely held together by the performance of its corporate religious rituals.[7]

If this is true of primitive civilizations, it is equally true of developed societies. Stancliffe's concern elsewhere in his essay is that we are in danger of losing this key facet of our corporate existence. More recently anthropologists have indicated how avowedly atheistic societies have found the need to generate "rites" at birth, and more notably for the onset of adolescence and the gateway into maturity. Confirmation, or in the Jewish tradition, the *Bar Mitzvah*, are replaced by a rite marking the onset of adulthood.[8] Stancliffe suggests that in different ways rituals are sought to replace worship, but that such rituals ignore the essential nature of that link with the unchanging reality upon which all depends. This is at the root of the impact of the *Book of Common Prayer* upon English society (and, through the Anglican Communion, upon other societies throughout the world) over the past 450 years.[9] If this is so, then what has this impact been and by which means has it been effected?

———

Already we have set out some of the aims both of Cranmer and of the 1662 revisers in putting together the *Book of Common Prayer*. In the stimulating introduction to his recent edition of the 1549, 1559, and 1662 texts of the *Book of Common Prayer*, Brian Cummings captures the impact of the book upon English society. He notes that:

> It came into being as a physical embodiment of a revolution in religious practice and in the politics of religion which we know as the Reformation, although even that term is a ragged shorthand for the domino of personal, communal, and national transformations which it provoked.[10]

It was thus:

> an engine of change, imposed on congregations and causing riots through its perverse assumption of doctrinal oddity and destruction of the old ways of experiencing the divine; yet also at the same time a vehicle for new forms of religious devotion and a brilliant literary achievement in its own right.[11]

As Cummings indicates, and as has been demonstrated by a number of revisionist Reformation historians, the English Reformation (or "Reformations"[12]) was not a popular movement issuing from a revolution amongst the common people, but rather a revolution imposed from above for both political and religious reasons.[13]

Cummings refers to Cranmer as " . . . a determined but temperamentally unzealous Reformer".[14] Not only was Cranmer an "unzealous Reformer", he was also eclectic in gathering from his various sources, which is partially what helped the English Reformation to appear idiorhythmic in contrast to that in other parts of northern Europe. So Peter Martyr, Jan Laski, and Martin Bucer were all welcomed to England. Bucer became Professor in Cambridge and Peter Martyr (Pietro Vermigli Martire) Professor in Oxford. Yet the Preface to the 1549 Book, already quoted, was based on the preface to the reformed breviary prepared by the Spanish Roman Catholic bishop, Cardinal Francisco Quiñones. This breviary had been prepared at the behest of Pope Clement VII and was published in 1535.[15] So Cranmer's sources were rich and various. In addition to this was the part played by the legislature. In developing the 1549 Book, one of the most extraordinary episodes was the debate in Parliament, which began on 19 December 1548. It was unique, even in an English Parliament, to debate the theology of the Eucharist and the meaning of the Latin words, "*Hoc est corpus meum*", "This is my body."[16] All this contributed to this formative and transformative book.

The publication of both the 1549 and 1552 Prayer Books was not the beginning of one constant religious and political order whereby English society would be fashioned. The Prayer Books experienced two exiles. The first was during the brief restoration of Roman jurisdiction under Mary Tudor, from 1553 to 1558. The second exile, between 1645 and 1662, marked an opposite swing of the pendulum during the seventeenth-century Puritan Revolution. Interestingly enough, however, by 1641 the Book had already "settled into the national consciousness", and Cummings reminds us that "the abolition of the Book of Common Prayer in 1645 was equally as political an act as its imposition had been in 1549."[17] The same would be true, once again, after the Restoration of the monarchy in 1660. At the Savoy Conference of 1661 John Cosin, the Bishop of Durham, was the key figure. He was a Laudian and would have taken the revised prayer book in that direction, but there were competing voices. Edward Reynolds, the Bishop of Norwich and author of the much acclaimed "General Thanksgiving", was effectively a Presbyterian, and so the final result of the Savoy Conference and the book which issued from it emerged in the form of another "political settlement". It fell to the traditionalist

Bishop of Lincoln, Robert Sanderson, a noted moral theologian, to write
the new preface. His introduction marks out the settlement very clearly:

> It hath been the wisdom of the Church of *England*, ever
> since the first compiling of her publick liturgy, to keep the
> mean between the two extremes, of too much stiffness in
> refusing, and of too much easiness in the admitting any
> variation from it.

So the preface begins. It ends on a suitably similar mollifying note:

> Yet we have good hope, that what is here presented and
> hath been by the Convocations of both Provinces with
> great diligence examined and approved, will also be well
> accepted and approved by all sober, peaceable, and truly
> conscientious Sons of the Church of *England*.

Mollifying as these words now read, and compromising as many would
see the 1662 *Book of Common Prayer* to have been, that was not the end of
the story in 1662. The book was accompanied by an Act of Uniformity. If
the Prayer Book was to be both a formative and a performative instrument
in the fashioning of English politics and piety, then it was clear that there
must be enforcement. Thus followed what was later described as the
"Great Ejection". Large numbers of ministers of a Presbyterian theological
position were effectively exiled from the "Church by law established".
Any reflection upon the formative nature of the *Book of Common Prayer*
must take into account those who were excluded—Puritans and Roman
Catholics—as well as the majority who were intended to be included.

In her seminal book on the impact of the *Book of Common Prayer* in
Elizabethan and early Stuart England, Judith Maltby focuses on just these
themes in the period before the Restoration and the publication of the
1662 Book. Early on she reflects:

> The role of liturgy as propaganda has been in large part
> overlooked—yet there was probably no other single aspect
> of the Reformation in England which touched more directly

and fundamentally the religious consciousness, or lack
of it, of ordinary clergy and laity, than did the reforms of
rituals and liturgy.[18]

Then just a little later:

... liturgy is an expression of a community's beliefs, as
well as a shaper of them. The relationship is a dynamic
and interdependent one; and one in which it is not always
possible to distinguish between cause and effect.[19]

Part of this propaganda included an intricate interweaving of the role of the
monarch, who in this new reformed church is the "Supreme Governor";
this is an integral part of the new polity. It is there throughout, but explicit
in the Communion rite in the Collect for the Monarch, to be said alongside
the Collect of the Day. It is there, too, in the overt references in the Prayer
for the Church Militant. The impact of such propaganda should not be
ignored; as we noted earlier, by the 1640s, the Prayer Book had gained a
key place in the religious consciousness of the people of England, hence
the division caused by those preparing the populace for the second exile
of the Book in 1645. Maltby notes:

A goodly proportion of the English people became "people
of the book"—but as much of the Prayer Book as of the
Bible. For conformists that association represented no
conflict, but rather a happy alliance at best, a manageable
partnership at worst.[20]

Conformity in this early "Prayer Book period" is the key focus of Maltby's
study and as such it explores developments in careful detail, using specific
local examples in Cheshire but also with reference to places elsewhere in
England. She notes that conformity drew support from a cross-section of
society.[21] Furthermore, she argues that the impact of conformity related
not only to religious matters but also to the maintenance of the fabric
of society as a whole.[22] This made the Prayer Book a key focus in the
religious controversies of seventeenth-century England; it also meant that

the settlement following the Restoration in 1660 had to be managed with great care. These sensibilities are clear in the politically couched language of Robert Sanderson's preface to the 1662 Book. They are also clear in the coercive implications of the new Act of Uniformity. In her conclusion, Maltby quotes John Spurr:

> For all the talk of Moses and Aaron, ministry and magistracy, alliance of altar and sword, the Church of England did not enjoy the committed support of the governors of England in the 1660s.[23]

The Church of England was formally restored to its place as the national church and this was enforced by law. Nonetheless, any monopoly would be short-lived on account of the energy and commitment of Christian dissenters. It was the "Glorious Revolution" of 1689 that would finally replace a "national" church with an "established" church[24] and allow more toleration for dissenters, albeit with significant continuing disabilities in public life, including education. These mixed developments require us to view the formative nature of the *Book of Common Prayer* on English life, from 1662 onwards, with a degree of subtlety. There is no doubting its impact, but the existence of a continuing recusant Roman Catholic minority and a robust group of Protestant dissenters meant that the Prayer Book's undoubted impact on public life and the formation of a "Christian society" was to be seen within this broader context. With Catholic emancipation in 1829, the influx of Irish immigrants following the famines of the 1840s, and also the rise of Methodism in the eighteenth century, the religious scene in England took on a more complex hue. Nonetheless, the predominance of the Church of England, its presence universal in country districts, and its relationship to the Establishment (and indeed its own *established* role) allowed the *Book of Common Prayer* to play a crucial and transformative role over the next three hundred years. The controversy surrounding attempts to revise the Book in the early twentieth century, exposed to detailed study in a later chapter, is testimony to the key influences still believed to issue from the *Book of Common Prayer* during the period right up to the outbreak of the Second World War.[25]

—

Apart from the conformity required by successive Acts of Uniformity, how and why has the *Book of Common Prayer* had the profound impact attributed to it by historical, sociological, and theological commentators? Parts of the answer to these questions have emerged incidentally already in this essay. One of the key factors was the publication of the liturgy in the vernacular. A number of scholars have referred to the implications of this key development and initiative going back to Cranmer's earliest work. David Loades, in stressing how the vernacular liturgy automatically made liturgy once again a collective act of worship, also draws out a political point. He argues that Cranmer's later revision of 1552 implicitly undermined the power of the clergy and gave more of a lever to laity in key positions in the nation, hence Loades comments:

> To the lay councillors imposing [the new liturgy], it represented a new structure of power, in which the church would be the department of state for ecclesiastical affairs, and the clergy would be civil servants.[26]

Politically sinister as this sounds, its positive implications have lived on despite all the vicissitudes of history that have intervened since that date. The Church of England continues to exercise this seminal role and it is fascinating that it is effectively a by-product of liturgical reform. In a speech at Lambeth Palace before a group of leaders from different religious faiths, the Queen reflected:

> Here at Lambeth Palace we should remind ourselves of the significant position of the Church of England in our nation's life. The concept of our established Church is occasionally misunderstood and, I believe, commonly under-appreciated. Its role is *not* to defend Anglicanism to the exclusion of other religions. Instead, the Church has a duty to protect the free practice of all faiths in this country.
>
> It certainly provides an identity and spiritual dimension for its own many adherents. But also, gently and assuredly,

the Church of England has created an environment for
other faith communities and indeed people of no faith
to live freely. Woven into the fabric of this country, the
Church has helped to build a better society—more and
more in active co-operation for the common good with
those of other faiths.[27]

Loades points to one of the springing points for this remarkable role
which would be assumed by the Church of England. It relates directly to
the earliest initiatives to publish a vernacular liturgy. Without a doubt
that same liturgical source has been one of the contributors to the "better
society" to which the Queen refers. The Queen also talks of the "fabric of
this country", thus picking up similar resonances to those of Judith Maltby
in her analysis of *The Book of Common Prayer* and early conformity.

Alongside the shift of the liturgy into the vernacular stands the issue
of how language is used. Rhetorical language is a key to this in conveying
theological truth. So Uwe Michael Lang writes:

Language is more than just a means of communication, it
is also a medium of expression. Human speech is not just
a utilitarian instrument that serves to communicate facts,
and should do so in the most simple and efficient manner.
It is also the means of expressing the workings of our mind
in a way that involves our whole personality.[28]

In his essay Lang is looking particularly at the role played by Latin in the
Roman liturgy, but he is also making a general point about the use of
language, and notably in the liturgy. Others point to a similar significance
of rhetoric in the *Book of Common Prayer*. Reflecting on the work of René
Girard, David Jasper notes:

The religious community, therefore, is bound upon the
wheel of a sacred rhetoric whose power is either a deception
or an absolute truth—the rhetoric allows no distinction to
be made.[29]

Jasper notes a little further on:

> It is clear from his work that Thomas Cranmer had learnt
> well the techniques of rhetoric which made up one third of
> the foundation course for undergraduates at the Cambridge
> of his day.[30]

Jasper argues that Cranmer makes good use of rhetoric which he mines
from the classical rather than the Jewish tradition. Sometimes the rhetoric
is hortatory. Such, he argues, is the first exhortation in the 1549 Book,
which he sees as powerful in its appeal for the people to approach the
sacrament with a penitent heart. Such use of rhetoric, Jasper argues,
allows "a breaking down and reconstituting of language deeper and more
recondite than is allowed by the extensive claims of recognised spirituality
and theology."[31] Jasper suggests there is almost a conspiratorial element
in Cranmer's use of language. For example, in the Prayer of Oblation in
the 1549 eucharistic rite, participants are made "to admit that they are,
in fact, unworthy to offer the sacrifice."[32]

Without using the language of conspiracy, Bridget Nichols also alludes
to Cranmer's evocative use of language in the liturgy. She argues that
such rhetoric is a product of his skill and creativity as a theologian and
writer: "[W]hat we have is Cranmer the liturgist quoting Cranmer the
translator", so she asks, "How far is it possible to say that skilful translation
and redeployment of original material is in itself a form of originality?"[33]
Nichols finds a positive answer in quoting the historical scholar (himself
a Roman Catholic), Eamon Duffy. Commenting on the 1973 translation
of the Roman Missal, Duffy notes:

> Time and again the versions in the *Book of Common Prayer*
> render virtually exactly and fully both the rhetorical force
> and the theological depth of the Latin originals. Time and
> again, alas, the 1973 English versions subvert both.[34]

What we discover in these reflections is that both the vernacular translation
with its corporate liturgical consequences, and the rhetorical use of
language—both hortatory and laudatory—have also contributed to the

impact of the *Book of Common Prayer* as an instrument in the "formation" of both English piety and polity. In two successive articles, Nichols, this time with Jeff Astley, spells out the formative nature of the Prayer Book. First, reflecting on the mention of the Prayer Book in literature and then alluding to the book's history, both the explicit and implicit educative impact of the book is explored. They note:

> Liturgy usually carries its learning lightly, "transforming a theology into the cry of a community". [*Again quoting Jasper.*] The learning that takes place through the liturgy works primarily through a *hidden curriculum* of learning experiences that are not overtly labelled as acts of teaching, but which are potentially much more significant than overtly didactic exposition. The formative power of the liturgy is largely implicit. We learn our Christianity on our knees and on our feet through saying and singing prayers and psalms (and, of course, hymns); as well as by sitting and listening to readings, sermons and—not often these days—exhortation.[35]

This brings us back to the earlier emphasis on the liturgy as a "divine given", as the *opus Dei*. The rhetoric is not merely in a self-conscious, humanly generated text. Instead, it issues from the tradition itself, including Holy Scripture. In the second of their two articles, Astley and Nichols move on to the *performative* nature of the liturgy, crucial to understanding the power and the influence of the *Book of Common Prayer*. So Astley and Nichols comment directly:

> Worship comes to life, and reveals its potential to form its participants, when it is performed.[36]

This is a thesis with a long history and once again it reinforces the divinely initiated element essential to the formative power of the liturgy upon both the Church itself and upon national life. It involves *mimesis*, that is a rehearsing of the tradition itself and thus of God's encounter with the community both within Holy Scripture and subsequently within the tradition and experience. So, for example, in the Communion rite, the essence of salvation history is iterated in the saving acts of God in Jesus. This understanding has been classically expressed by Erich Auerbach and his argument is essential to this aspect of the Prayer Book's formative power. Auerbach argues that mimesis is crucial for understanding *scriptural* texts. The issue there is not about "crude history" but instead the performative living out of the truth. On scriptural narrative he notes that:

> ... the moral, religious, and psychological phenomena which are their sole concern are made concrete in the sensible matter of life.[37]

Within the *Book of Common Prayer*, then, it is the liturgy performed that is transformative; it is a mimetic process.

—

In what sense, then, has the *Book of Common Prayer*, over the past 350 years (or perhaps more accurately 460 years) been transformative? How has it animated those who for one reason or another would describe themselves as Anglican? Anglican and Anglicanism have come to have a technical meaning in both ecclesiology and in ecclesiastical history; use of these terms is now almost universally assumed to relate to the churches or provinces of the Anglican Communion. Used in this technical sense it has a comparatively short history, perhaps to be traced back to the mid-nineteenth century and effectively to 1867, when Archbishop Longley convened the first Lambeth Conference largely in response to the Colenso crisis in South Africa.[38]

The term Anglican, however, could be said to have an older and more diffuse meaning in more direct relationship to the Church of England.[39] Often the English ecclesiastical tradition is paired with the phrase "*Ecclesia Anglicana*". Here it describes the essential qualities that have defined the western catholic inheritance as it was received and developed in England, both pre- and post-Reformation. It might be used in parallel with the term Gallican, which refers to the distinctive tradition of the western Catholic Church in France. In that sense, "Anglican" can refer both technically to that family of churches which make up the Anglican Communion worldwide, but also to the distinctive nature of the way the Church of God has manifested itself in England, and to a certain degree in the Church of England. If this double identity holds water, then it could be said that, since the Reformation, it is the *Book of Common Prayer* that has animated both senses of the word Anglican. In different ways, the *Book of Common Prayer* (which has, as this present volume demonstrates, experienced its own internal development) has animated both Anglicanisms. The family of churches which form the Anglican Communion all owe their initial identity, either directly or indirectly, to the fashioning power of the *Book of Common Prayer*.[40]

Animation is itself patient of at least two different definitions. The first is simply to give life to something or someone. The second is the rather more specific meaning relating to the Latin word "*anima*" which is the word translated into English as "soul". Giving *soul* to something implies more than life and suggests a spiritual depth. So, for example, there has been talk of generating a real sense of spirituality in relation to the European Union and the nations which comprise it. The call has been for the discovery of a "Soul for Europe". In both these senses, the *Book of Common Prayer* has been responsible for the animation of the churches of the Anglican Communion and also in what it has given to England, through the Church and as a nation, over a period of at least 400 years. Something of both these is conveyed in the introduction to Brian Cummings' new edition of the Books of 1549, 1559 and 1662. He writes:

> More than a book of devotion, then, this is a book to live, love, and die to.

and then later:

> It is a book of ritual, of practices and performances used to transform the activities of a life. Rituals, anthropologists now tell us, are what make the human animal different. Mankind is a "ceremonial animal", Wittgenstein said. Ritual is the social act basic to humanity, the means by which we draw our lives together into a mutual practice.[41]

This brings together so much of our earlier argument in relation to the *Book of Common Prayer* and its formative impact on English society: mimetic, performative, social, and the ritual which makes us human, to which Michael Stancliffe's essay directed us. The *Book of Common Prayer* is a text, but more than that, it is a performative text. This is true in as much as it is not simply a book of words. Instead these words are to be performed as liturgy; they are the basis for a series of rituals; they are in essence the script for a drama.[42] In the eucharistic rite the entire mystery of salvation is rehearsed every time the rite is celebrated. But it is not somehow rehearsed in isolation from the rest of our lives. It informs all that we do and are, and it also calls out of us a response. The word liturgy, deriving from the Greek word *leitourgia* (λειτουργία) has the resonance of *service* held within its meaning. Later in his essay, Michael Stancliffe writes of the primitive Church:

> That does not mean, as the New Testament makes clear, that the early Christians passed their days mooning about in a pious dream, mumbling prayers and abstractedly doing their jobs with their hands while their minds were fixed on heaven. Very much the reverse. They celebrated perpetually in and through the service of their fellow men. That word "service" means quite literally "the work of a servant"— feeding the hungry, caring for the sick, supporting the weak, comforting the afflicted. That service was all part of the ritual, all part of the continuously repeated pattern of action and word whereby they celebrated the words and deeds of their Master and set forward the coming of his kingdom.[43]

But those texts which relate to rites of passage are also performative in an equally profound sense. In the rites of baptism, confirmation, holy matrimony, and the burial of the dead, they especially focus Cummings' phrase of the book being "a book to live, love, and die to." The fact that the texts themselves emerged from a long and complex process, over a period of more than a century, and even requiring debate in Parliament, gives them a currency well beyond the devotional scripts for those who choose to be there regularly worshipping in church. They are scripts that have underlain the growth of our culture over a period of 400 years, including two periods when the book was in exile. Even in 1928, the proposals for a new revised prayer book were sharply debated in both Houses of Parliament.

The performative nature of the Prayer Book rites runs at two different levels. First, as we have argued, they capture key moments in the lives of individuals, families, and communities. They act as rites of passage. So the calling of Banns of Marriage still reminds us that marriage is the property not only of the couple, but also of the wider community. Equally, within the rite, the responsibility of the community is underscored: "Therefore if any man can show any just cause why they may not lawfully be joined together, let him now speak, or else hereafter for ever hold his peace." This follows the preface which sets out the reasons for marriage and also a pattern of life destined to nurture a healthy society. The promises required of the couple are equally rich in setting a pattern for the flourishing of family life: "Wilt thou love her, comfort her, honour and keep her, so long as you both shall live?" Then, moments later, "With this ring I thee wed, with my body I thee worship, and with all my worldly goods I thee endow . . ."

That this is part of an unfolding of an *entire life* lived in the presence of God is made clear in the earlier rite of passage, that of confirmation. The words pronounced by the bishop at the laying on of hands run, "Defend, O Lord, this thy Child (or this thy *Servant*) with thy heavenly grace, that *he* may continue thine for ever: and daily increase in thy holy Spirit more and more, until *he* come unto thy everlasting kingdom. Amen." The *Book of Common Prayer* sets out a pattern for the whole of life which is implied to be a continuous journey, so we "daily increase in thy holy Spirit more and more". At the burial of the dead this same pattern is implied: "In the midst of life we are in death: of whom may we seek for succour, but of thee, O Lord, who for our sins art justly displeased." As Cummings puts it, Cranmer did not coin the words, "In the midst of life we are in death."; but he knew them from the inside, and he allowed them to live in others after him.[44]

Alongside these rites of passage, we should not forget one other remarkable innovation of the *Book of Common Prayer*. Cranmer was determined, as we have seen from the 1549 Preface, that his book should be accessible and thus formative of all people. He thus condensed the monastic hours of prayer into two offices for the morning and the evening, with a pattern of prayer which recited the entire Psalter within the mornings and evenings of one month. The saying of these offices remains a requirement for all Church of England clergy, but far more than just those who are ordained regularly say these offices. Sometimes in twos and threes, lay people faithfully say Morning and Evening Prayer in parish churches in town and country throughout England. In cathedrals and in many college chapels the offices have been sung every evening for 450 years except for the break in the Commonwealth period.

So all these offices, prayers, and rites are performative, too, of the story which is the foundation and framework of the Christian tradition which has helped shape European and English culture. In this sense, as Auerbach argues, they are mimetic.[45] Each rite rehearses in different ways elements of the story of Jesus Christ and of the religious culture from which that story sprang. Such performance and mimesis has been a powerful influence on the fashioning of our society. Modern linguistics has shown how crucial the structure, grammar, and syntax of language are in fashioning human relationships and community.[46] Mimetic rehearsal of such language and texts plays a key role in the self-understanding of a community and nation. The significance of the *Book of Common Prayer*, then, extends well beyond our admiring it as a piece of linguistic construction. This also suggests that what we now call "public theology", that is, the influence of religious faith in the political arena, will have been fashioned through the key part played in English culture by the *Book of Common Prayer*.[47] The cadences of the Prayer Book echo down the centuries. Let the final word on formation and transformation rest with Brian Cummings:

> Some of the praises of the book, of the glories of its language, have been misplaced. It is not a special form of language; it is the ordering language of its time, the vocabulary of the mid-sixteenth century, overlaid with the rhythm of the mid-seventeenth. Yet it is a language with an unmistakeable power, employed freely by all other users of the English language, whatever their religious affiliation or whether

they have one at all. Winnie, in Samuel Beckett's *Happy Days*, contemplates the absurdity and futility of her life in the jetsam of her handbag, all the odds and ends spread out before her. "For Jesus Christ sake Amen," she says: "World without end Amen."[48]

NOTES

1. First published as "All Such Good Works: The Book of Common Prayer & the Fashioning of English Society", in Stephen G. Platten and Christopher Woods (eds.), *Comfortable Words: Polity, Piety and the Book of Common Prayer* (SCM Press, 2012), ISBN 9780334046707; reproduced here by kind permission of the publisher (<https://www.scmpress.co.uk>).

2. Cf. here David Loades, "The Revision of the Prayer Book in 1552" in David Loades (ed.), *Word and Worship: Essays Presented to Margot Johnson* (Davenant Press, 2005), p. 78. See also C. S. Lewis, *English Literature in the Sixteenth Century: Excluding Drama* (Clarendon Press, 1954), especially pp. 215–221. And also Rowan Williams, *Christmas Day Sermon*, 2011: at one point, the then Archbishop noted, of the impact of the 1662 *Book of Common Prayer*, "It has shaped the minds and hearts of millions; and it has done so partly because it has never been a book for individuals alone. It is common prayer, prayer that is shared." (<http://rowanwilliams.archbishopofcanterbury.org/articles.php/2292/archbishops-christmas-sermon-dont-build-lives-on-selfishness-and-fear>).

3. On this see, for example, Christopher Irvine, *The Art of God: The Making of Christians and the Meaning of Worship* (SPCK, 2005).

4. Transliterated into modern English for ease of reading.

5. Michael Stancliffe, "The Substance of Worship" (unpublished essay, delivered to the Annual Ministry Conference of the Diocese of Portsmouth, 5 January 1985), p. 5.

6. Ibid.

7. Ibid., pp. 8–9. Cf. also John Macmurray, "The Celebration of Communion", Chapter vii in his *Persons in Relation* (Faber and Faber, 1961).

8. So here cf. James Thrower, *Marxism-Leninism as the Civil Religion of Soviet Society: God's Commissar* (Edwin Mellen Press, 1992).

9. Cf. here Rowan Williams, "Imagining the Kingdom: Some Questions for Anglican Worship Today", in Kenneth Stevenson and Bryan Spinks (eds.), *The Identity of Anglican Worship* (Mowbray, 1991), p. 8. " . . . it is the Communion Order of 1549, 1552 and 1662 that most clearly sets out the 'public' and social dimensions of belonging to the Body of Christ, since it is precisely at the Lord's Table that the congregation is called to answer for the life of the community."

10. Brian Cummings (ed.), *The Book of Common Prayer: The Texts of 1549, 1559, and 1662* (Oxford University Press, 2011), p. xiii.

11. Ibid.

12. Christopher Haigh, *English Reformations: Religion, Politics, and Society Under the Tudors* (Clarendon Press, 1993).

13. Note here particularly Eamon Duffy, *The Stripping of the Altars: Traditional Religion in England, c.1400-c.1580* (Yale University Press, 1992). But cf. also Diarmaid MacCulloch, *Tudor Church Militant: Edward VI and the Protestant Reformation* (Allen Lane, 1999).

14. Cummings, *The Book of Common Prayer*, p. xx.

15. Ibid., p. 689.

16. Ibid., p. xxv.

17. Ibid., p. xli.

18. Judith Maltby, *Prayer Book and People in Elizabethan and Early Stuart England* (Cambridge University Press, 1998), p. 4.

19. Ibid.

20. Ibid., p. 17.

21. Ibid., p. 24.

22. Ibid., for example, pp. 170–172.

23. Ibid., p. 233, quoting John Spurr, *The Restoration Church of England 1646–1689* (Yale University Press, 1991), p. 59.

24. Ibid., p. 235.

25. For detailed explanation of the controversy over the "deposited" 1928 Prayer Book, see Donald Gray, *The 1927–28 Prayer Book Crisis 1, Ritual, Royal Commissions, and Reply to the Royal Letters of Business*, and *The 1927–28 Prayer Book Crisis 2, The cul-de-sac of the* Deposited Book . . . *until further order be taken, Joint Liturgical Studies* 60 and 61 (SCM-Canterbury Press, Alcuin Club, GROW, 2005, 2006).

26. Loades, "The Revision of the Prayer Book in 1552", p. 83.

27. Speech by HM Queen Elizabeth II at Lambeth Palace, Wednesday 15 February 2012 (<http://rowanwilliams.archbishopofcanterbury.org/articles.php/2358/hm-the-queen-attends-multi-faith-reception>).

28. Uwe Michael Lang, "Rhetoric of Salvation: The Origins of Latin as the Language of the Roman Liturgy" in Uwe Michael Lang (ed.), *The Genius of the Roman Rite: Historical, Theological, and Pastoral Perspectives on Catholic Liturgy* (Hillenbrand Books, 2009).

29. David Jasper, *Rhetoric, Power and Community: An Exercise in Reserve* (Macmillan, 1993), p. 78.

30. Ibid.

31. Ibid., p. 84.

32. Ibid., p. 85.

33. Bridget Nichols, "Cranmer's Intolerable Burdens: Plagiarism, Appreciation or Originality", in *In Illo Tempore: Ushaw Library Bulletin and Liturgical Review* No. 9 (August 1999), p. 13.

34. Ibid., p. 14, quoting Duffy, "Rewriting the Liturgy: The Theological Implications of Translation" in Stratford Caldecott (ed.), *Beyond the Prosaic: Renewing the Liturgical Movement* (Black, 1998), p. 110.

35. Jeff Astley and Bridget Nichols, "The Formative Role of the Book of Common Prayer", in *Prayer Book Society Journal* (Trinity 2011), p. 9.

36. Ibid.

37. Erich Auerbach, *Mimesis: The Representation of Reality in Western Literature* (Princeton University Press, 1991), p. 14. See also Stephen Platten, "Liturgical Living: Learning by Mimesis", in *Anaphora* Vol. 5 Part 1 (June 2011), pp. 23–38 (and in this book, Chapter 7).

38. W. M. Jacob, *The Making of the Anglican Church Worldwide* (SPCK, 1997), pp. 158 ff.

39. Cf. here references in Maltby, *Prayer Book and People*, p. 9, and *ad loc.*

40. This has been demonstrated and researched comprehensively in Charles Hefling and Cynthia Shattuck (eds.), *The Oxford Guide to The Book of Common Prayer: A Worldwide Survey* (Oxford University Press, 2006). There is not space in this chapter to develop this area, which is well covered in the volume noted above. Cf. Christopher Irvine (ed.), *Anglican Liturgical Identity: Joint Liturgical Study* No. 65 (Canterbury Press, Alcuin Club, GROW, 2008).

41. Cummings, *The Book of Common Prayer*, p. xii.

42. Ibid., p. li. Cummings quotes the liturgical scholar Gregory Dix: " . . . rite is not speech alone. It is 'primarily something done', not said."

43. Stancliffe, "The Substance of Worship", pp. 14–15.

44. Cummings, *The Book of Common Prayer*, p. li.

45. Auerbach, *Mimesis, ad loc.*

46. Diarmaid MacCulloch, *Thomas Cranmer: A Life* (Yale University Press, 1996), p. 631.

47. Richard Harries and Stephen Platten (eds.), *Reinhold Niebuhr and Contemporary Politics: God and Power* (Oxford University Press, 2010). See in particular Stephen Platten, "Niebuhr, Liturgy, and Public Theology" (Chapter 7), and Chapter 10 in this volume.

48. Cummings, *The Book of Common Prayer*, p. lii.

9.   THE USES OF LITURGY: WORSHIP NOURISHING MISSION[1]

In 1957, Richard Hoggart published one of the most influential sociological essays of twentieth-century Britain. Entitled *The Uses of Literacy*,[2] it effectively became iconic for its age and is still in print, fifty years later. The book's analysis has been significant at a number of different but related levels. First of all, it establishes the importance of literacy in opening up new worlds to far broader audiences. The ability to read, and more particularly to read sophisticated and imaginative literature, transformed the horizons of countless people who, in an earlier generation, would not have benefited from similar opportunities. It has become almost a commonplace to say that "knowledge is power"; that is, the more we know, the more likely we are to be able to unlock new possibilities and to open ourselves up to broader and richer aspirations within our lives. If, however, knowledge is power, then pressing the argument further, literacy is also power, for literacy effectively unlocks knowledge. This point received added potency in Hoggart's book, since he, rather like playwright Alan Bennett, came from a working class background in Leeds and, through a grammar school education, went on to become Professor of English in the University of Birmingham, and ultimately Warden of Goldsmith's College in the University of London. In a prophetic way, remembering some of the problems which arose through the move to comprehensive secondary education, Hoggart wrote:

> The examination at eleven-plus may be in many things
> clumsy, but it does with a fair measure of success select
> intellectually agile children.[3]

We cannot, however, engage further in this controversy here. Ironically, comprehensive education rooted in neighbourhood schools has undermined that positive process. Hoggart also develops his argument in another direction. Having spent some time on what he calls the "earnest minority"—that particularly is those working-class families and children who benefit through hitherto unknown possibilities for literacy—he is clear that this new literacy has its dangers too. So he notes:

> The "earnest minority" is very important, but it would be a
> mistake to allow the discussion of their situation to close a
> book chiefly concerned with attitudes among a majority.[4]

This leads him to reflect upon what he calls popular publications. Here he notes:

> As we study popular publications we insensibly tend to give
> them, so great is their mere bulk, a larger prominence in
> the whole pattern of people's experience than, in fact, they
> have. In the areas in which they have their most intensive
> effect, that effect can be harmful: over some wider aspects
> of experience, they may have some adverse effect too . . . [5]

This leads him to warn that the literacy explosion can be partly the cause of the debasing of standards of social behaviour and then lead to real dangers within our society. So the uses of literacy are not only very significant, but they may have an ambiguous effect. Standards of publication within literature are important if literacy is to deepen and enrich our society. This is why Allen Lane's initiative in setting up Penguin Books, pioneering a high quality paperback list, was so significant,[6] as indeed was the setting up by Boots the Chemist of their "Booklovers Libraries".

There is one further educational footnote which should be added here. In the 1960s and 1970s, Basil Bernstein, Professor of the Sociology of

Education in the University of London, developed a theory of linguistic codes which further elaborates the argument set out above. He talks of two main linguistic codes which he calls "restricted" and "elaborated".[7] In short, in his argument we find that the restricted code is largely prevalent in working-class culture. It is terse, generally clear, and economic, but it takes for granted much that is unspoken. The elaborated code is a middle-class phenomenon and is more sophisticated, with complicated sentence structure using a wider vocabulary of words less commonly used; nothing is left unexplained. The implications of this research are again fairly clear. If much of society's more influential dialogue is couched in elaborated code, then those accustomed only to the terseness of the restricted code may find themselves at a disadvantage. At the very least, some sort of bridging mechanism may be necessary. Bernstein builds upon this point and its educational implications in a later essay.[8]

The reason for calling this chapter "The Uses of Liturgy" may now begin to become clearer. Without a good standard of literacy people can easily find themselves to be victims of real deprivation. The same charge of deprivation can be argued about religion and—more specifically—about Christianity which lacks adequate liturgy, or indeed human life which is bereft of a liturgical dimension. The liturgy is the one point at which people definitely have contact with the Church. This is true on a number of different levels. So, for regular churchgoers, the liturgy is the one place where we know they will have contact with the faith. Not all church members attend home groups or house groups, let alone lectures and specialist courses. All do, however, encounter God in the liturgy. What does that encounter do and say to them? Then again, fewer children now attend Sunday Schools and similar activities. The vast majority of children, however, do attend an act of worship in school; in a huge number of cases (even within state/community schools), clergy take part regularly, sometimes once a week. In yet a different context, large numbers of people encounter the Church through baptisms and weddings, and indeed the majority of the population do so through funerals. Once again, what do these liturgies say both to the un-churched majority and to those on the fringe?

Often a wedge is driven between liturgy and mission. Remembering what has been set out above, mission and liturgy stand or fall together.

Within the Christian tradition there has always been an unwillingness to allow the liturgy to become instrumental or indeed utilitarian. The liturgy is the *opus Dei*, the work of God. We offer it as our response to God's unconditional grace; it effectively forms part of the covenant of grace and love, responding to the God who comes among us in Jesus Christ. What we have seen hinted at so far, however, is not liturgy as a utilitarian exercise but instead liturgy as part of the air that we breathe. It is a language and grammar that *underpin* our living, learning, and confidence in *the faith*.

Richard Hoggart's reflections on literacy and society can now be seen to be highly illuminating. As with language and society, so with liturgy and Christian faith. Without worship and the liturgy we are deprived of the basic language of faith. Furthermore—and Bernstein's research comes into play here—poor liturgy, and liturgy starved of the basic images and stories underpinning the Christian faith, will not provide the grammar and vocabulary necessary for a healthy and intelligent life in the faith. This is true both of the solid core of Christian believers and, indeed, of those on the fringe or the un-churched, who encounter the faith only through the occasional offices. Liturgy and mission cannot survive without each other. As has already been hinted, this has implications in three different but related ways: liturgy has a direct impact upon our *knowledge* of the faith, our *confidence* in the faith, and our *living* of the faith. Let us take each of these in turn.

—

We shall begin, then, with knowledge of the faith. It is easy to take for granted the process generally given the shorthand name of "secularization". We can easily assume that since the 1960s there has been a sudden and dramatic exit from the Christian church of most of the population. This is the result, we are told, of secularization. Now the theory of secularization has itself sustained very significant criticism in recent years.[9] This, however, is not the point to enter that controversy. It is clear that in Britain the number attending churches has fallen significantly. Nevertheless this process actually goes back a very long way. Those of us who are old enough to have grandparents born in the last decades of the nineteenth century will know that, often, they were not regular churchgoers. The drift from regular churchgoing has a long history. Nevertheless, despite this drift, those same grandparents often still knew the basics of Christian faith. Sometimes it may have been transmitted to them through Sunday School. Often that transmission came via hymns and Christmas carols; my maternal grandmother could remember word for word "While Shepherds Watched" and "Once in Royal David's City", along with "O God, Our Help in Ages Past" and, indeed, several other popular hymns.

So perhaps the contrast that this highlights is not the rather obvious (and sometimes erroneous) point about secularization and churchgoing. Instead, it is about simple factual knowledge of the Christian faith and the key stories behind it, in both the Old and New Testaments. Grandma Sheward, known for her familiarity with carols and hymns, learnt too the stories of salvation history, from Jacob to Solomon, and the parables and miracles of Jesus too. She would often recite some of this, keen that I should know it too. More to the point, she learnt them both in Sunday School and through her divinity lessons at a Central London church school, St Gabriel in Pimlico. Even though she left school when she was fourteen years old, or possibly younger, the basic stories of the faith were bound fast within her mind.

This point is vividly clear in the literature of the time. Thomas Hardy, often chosen as an exemplar of Victorian agnosticism or even atheism, peppered his novels with scriptural allusions. Often names were biblical, but more than this, in his novels and poetry an intricate knowledge of the Old and New Testaments makes itself manifest again and again. It is Bathsheba Everdene who is the main character in *Far from the Madding Crowd*. As with King David, in the Old Testament succession narrative, so with Sergeant Troy, Farmer Boldwood, and Gabriel Oak; she carries the shadow of the temptress. Often too, in this novel and others, resonances of the *Book of Common Prayer* peep through again and again. Despite his ambiguous relationship with the Christian faith, Hardy exemplified the knowledge held by most country people, and many in the towns, at this time. His own Bible is annotated from beginning to end, indicating very frequent use.

In another very different and far more self-consciously autobiographical piece of literature, the same point shines through clearly. In *Lark Rise to Candleford*, Flora Thompson describes the rural England of her childhood in the 1880s and 1890s. Brought up on the boundaries of Oxfordshire and Northamptonshire, she was the daughter of a stonemason, and they lived for much of Flora's childhood in the "end cottage" in the hamlet of Juniper Hill, south of Brackley. Hers was a humble childhood by any standards. Albert, her father, unquestionably the weaker of her two parents, was—rather unusually—an agnostic, although he knew enough of the faith; Albert was an angry and resentful man who became increasingly keen on strong drink. Her mother came from a more conventionally "Church" family; she had also benefited from a little more education. Flora's biographer writes of her mother:

> Emma went to the rectory every day after school; there she was not only taught to sing but also to copy Miss Lowe's [the Rector's sister's] lovely eighteenth-century handwriting and her graceful old-fashioned manners. Emma could not fail to see the contrast between the dignified and cultured way of life at the rectory and her own home in the crowded cottage by the church. The experience taught her standards which she was to pass on to her daughter Flora.[10]

Flora was nurtured in this atmosphere and, despite the humble nature of her village schooling, she developed a remarkable love for literature and for writing herself. She read voraciously any book she could obtain. So the Bible was a mainstay, as was *Pilgrim's Progress*. At school she won the diocesan prize. This capacity for reading and this continuing thirst for more would follow Flora throughout her life. Rather like my grandmother, Flora left school at the age of fourteen and went to work in the village Post Office in Fringford, just a few miles away from Juniper Hill. One of her mother's friends ran the Post Office and she needed an assistant; she thought Emma's oldest daughter might be the right person for the job. She left home, never to return permanently, lodging with Kesia Whitton, her mother's friend and the postmistress. She gave much of her life to working but it was through her writing that she derived her real satisfaction.

Apart from her facility in written English, Flora's remarkable achievement was to have observed and then chronicled rural life, at Juniper Hill and in the nearby towns and villages, in the dying years of the nineteenth century. *Lark Rise* (the first of the trilogy which makes up *Lark Rise to Candleford*) was not published until 1939. Flora would only outlive its publication another eight years, dying at Dartmouth in South Devon in 1947. What is interesting is how her early education in the Christian faith, in the school and at church, would form her life. She remained a devout member of the Church of England until her death. Early on she writes:

> At a confirmation class which Laura [the pseudonym she chooses for herself in her books] attended, the clergyman's daughter, after weeks of careful preparation, asked her catechumens: "Now, are you sure you are all of you thoroughly prepared for tomorrow? Is there anything you would like to ask me?"[11]

Later on, Flora sets the scene in relation to the Church still more vividly. Rather as we have seen already, churchgoing was nothing like universal, even though through the intermittent contact with the Church, people would learn of the faith. So Flora writes:

> If the Lark Rise people had been asked their religion, the answer of nine out of ten would have been "Church of England", for practically all of them were christened, married, and buried as such, although in adult life, few went to church between the baptisms of their offspring.[12]

With great attractiveness Flora describes the scene in church without offering cynical reflections. So she comments:

> The psalms were not sung or chanted, but read, verse and verse about, by the Rector and people, and in these especially Tom's voice so drowned the subdued murmur of his fellow worshippers that it sounded like a duet between him and the clergyman . . . [13]

And then to the sermons:

> Mr Ellison in the pulpit was the Mr Ellison of the Scripture
> lessons [at school], plus a white surplice. To him, his
> congregation were but children of a large growth, and he
> preached as he taught. A favourite theme was the duty of
> regular churchgoing. He would hammer away at that for
> forty-five minutes, never seeming to realise that he was
> preaching to the absent, that all those present were regular
> attendants, and that the stray sheep of his flock were snoring
> upon their beds a mile and a half away. Another favourite
> subject was the supreme rightness of the social order as it
> then existed.[14]

Flora describes the Methodists too, and revivalist preachers. She writes
also of the Rector visiting each cottage in turn and of his kindliness despite
his "autocratic ideas". She writes, later, of the arrival of an Anglo-Catholic
Rector and of her mother's preference for plain and wholesome religion
"as the food she cooked". Despite the musty and dull feel of the religion
of her childhood, and indeed the unacceptable aspects of the various
rectors' admonitions, the whole of Flora's trilogy is interwoven with the
way in which the simplest of Christian teaching somehow permeated the
whole of the hamlet, and later on the wider world. As children, if at no
other time, all would encounter the faith. Part of it was caught up into folk
religion, described unforgettably in her chapter on the "Harvest Home".
That chapter ends with a sobering paragraph, remembering that Flora
was writing some fifty years after the events:

> And all the time boys were being born or growing up in the
> parish, expecting to follow the plough all their lives, or, at
> most, to do a little mild soldiering or go to work in a town.
> Gallipoli? Kut? Vimy Ridge? Ypres? What did they know of
> such places? But they were to know them. A brass plate on
> the wall of the church immediately over the old end house
> seat is engraved with their names. A double column, five
> names long, then, last and alone, the name of Edmund.[15]

Edmund, Flora's brother, is a poignant character from a world now lost which Flora describes. Even the reflections on Edmund's death in the Great War retain resonances of the religion which Flora had effectively drunk in from her mother's womb. Beautiful as is Flora's prose, she does not romanticize that lost world: at times she is sharply critical of its values. Nor, indeed, should this analysis romanticize the religion. It is certainly not reclaimable, nor would we wish it so except as part of a period drama or tableau. It does, however, indicate how, at least in childhood, all learnt the stories and experienced the cult (as it was then) which formed them in some sort of faith, even if, as is now still more the case, that religion was practised vicariously by a minority on behalf of a majority. What, then, might we learn about *knowledge* of the faith from this historical vignette? Perhaps most essentially it speaks to us of making the best of the opportunities which are presented to us. Flora Thompson's world saw people fashioned in the faith in their childhood in a bare and, to us, unattractive liturgy. But still it formed them. Starting with the core of the faithful, how do we do the same? Our knowledge and understanding of worship has been extraordinarily changed in the past generation or two. Older people still remember nothing other than the *Book of Common Prayer* or possibly the *English Missal*. People and churches were even referred to as "Prayer Book Catholic" or as "Matins Low Church People".

The liturgical revolution has reminded us that worship is not simply words, but a drama partially clothed in words. The story which stands at the centre of our faith, of our crucified and resurrected Lord, is the mystery at the heart of all things. It is that story which gives flesh to God. Somehow we must enact that mystery so that, by regular re-presentation of it, all of us grow in and deepen our faith. It will require words—scripture, preaching, and prayer—but it first and foremost requires us to tell the story with vigour and imagination, yet also with solemnity. Dom Odo Casel, the great twentieth-century Benedictine liturgical theologian, was clear that our weekly, or even daily, submergence in the mystery *forms* us as Christian people so that our very lives make us missionary in all our encounters.

But then there is also that series of occasional offices when both the fringe and the un-churched encounter God. Or do they? Sometimes they encounter only the Church or, worse still, only the institution. How can we tell the story and reveal something of the cult in baptisms? Can we not use pilgrimage and movement to more effect? After all, baptism is taking us down into the tomb and raising us with Christ. Can our imagery make that clear? The branch of rosemary soaking a congregation and reminding all of baptism can say more than hundreds of words. Or what of giving a crucifix to godparents or to those confirmed or baptized? That takes the story of what they experienced in the liturgy into their homes. If not a crucifix, then possibly an icon.

With marriage, how can sensitive preparation, rooted in a dialogue with the liturgy, speak of lives patterned on Christ and help express the unity that is intended and created by the natural sacramental rite of matrimony? Can a careful choreography of the rite itself, along with guidance in planning the rite, speak to all who are there? In orthodoxy, the vivid scene of husband and wife being crowned by God speaks richly of God's blessing on all of us.

Then to funerals and requiems. Here the resonances with the story of Jesus, and indeed of his own encounters with death, offer many possibilities. Of course, we need to embrace this with sensitivity. Mourners and families are not consumers to be offered a product that rather shallowly assuages grief. Instead, they are actors within the universal divine-human drama where Jesus, the incarnate one, has brought God into the centre of our lives and our being. Careful use of text, and even here of appropriate movement, can say much. Symbolism with water is again a potent reminder of God's embracing all in baptism. Each of these occasions may speak more of the story of God in Jesus Christ, which is knowledge of the faith.

—

If fewer people are in church it easily undermines an appropriate *confidence* that the Christian community should have in their faith. Confidence is not to be confused with hubris nor with a dishonest suppression of all doubt. But the overwhelming sense that worship is a minority interest, or the preserve of a marginalized sub-culture, is an easy feeling to develop for us, both as individuals and as a community. Many of us spend most of our lives engaging with people in secular occupations and in the everyday world. It is easy to assume, then, that most people in that wider context are, at the very least, uninterested in the faith, and at the worst, hostile to it.

As a clergyman or woman working in the secular world it is still easier to make this assumption. Doesn't my "habit" or "uniform" cause others either to cower or present an aggressive pose? Surely they won't want to work with me? In so many cases the very opposite is true. The vast majority of people we encounter are positively responsive. They may not immediately want to go to church, or indeed wish you to press them in that direction. They will, however, be sympathetic to the aims of the gospel and—if the opinion polls bear any accuracy—would see themselves as tacit believers. This is an important truth to grasp, since an assumption that all are against us, or certainly indifferent, can lead to a defensiveness within the Church. That either makes us deny our own title deeds, that is, the truths of our faith, or equally unhelpfully it can allow us to approach them with an aggressive stance; almost always when we refer to people acting defensively, in reality it communicates itself as aggression!

The significance of an appropriate confidence in the faith, and indeed of the richness of our faith, has been vividly expressed in a recent novel. In *Miss Garnet's Angel*,[16] Salley Vickers engages with a woman who has just reached retirement and who has decided to take an exciting holiday with the companion with whom she has shared a house for many years. As we read on, this venture seems unlikely in itself, for Miss Garnet is described as a very dry old stick. She comes from a non-believing family of the utmost seriousness. She is herself an atheist and has been bound up with a series of high-minded causes throughout her life—the Campaign for Nuclear Disarmament and other similar political activities. These pursuits, however, have increased her dryness rather than enriched her personality. When she comes to book her much heralded holiday, her friend has sadly died before they can go. But Miss Garnet remains true to her promise to her friend and she decides on Venice for her exciting destination, and exciting it certainly turns out to be.

Rather than ruin the novel for future readers, a few reflections will make the point. One of the stories that Miss Garnet discovers in her journeying is that of Tobias and the Angel, found in the Apocrypha. The presence of angels thereafter becomes a theme for her transformed life. Miss Garnet discovers the power of love which releases her for the way in which she now responds to other people. But it also speaks in her of a feeling for, and an understanding of, the transcendent. It is a beautifully told story and it stimulates both one's thought and emotions. It has a clear message for those who already have a religious sensitivity, and for those for whom religion has not been a prime concept or even experience. Certainly for those who are religiously sensitive it is capable of reviving or strengthening an appropriate confidence in the faith.

Then again, Salley Vickers' most recent novel, *The Other Side of You*, is similarly encouraging for those with or without a religious sensitivity. This time the novel focuses upon a psychotherapist and his relationship with one of his clients. Some similar sensitivities are kindled, but this time starting from a quite different point of origin. Again it touches upon religious belief and this time the theme running alongside is the artist Caravaggio and his work. One brief couplet in particular captures this issue of confidence. The couplet runs thus:

> B: But belief can't alter the physical
>   substance of the world?
> A: It can alter people's perception of it. Belief does alter
>   people, marvellously, if only they'll believe it.[17]

The point arising from both these novels is the effect of the transcendent upon one's understanding of the meaning of human life. Prayer, contemplation, and worship—and all arise by implication in both novels— can change people's perceptions and so their lives. Liturgy lies at the centre of this, as we have seen from Odo Casel's contribution to liturgical theology. Liturgy and the practice of worship is central in nourishing an appropriate sense of confidence in religious faith: "Belief does alter people, marvellously, if only they'll believe it."[18] This marvellous piece of irony moves us on to the third use of liturgy, *living the faith*.

———

Amongst contemporary American novelists, Anne Tyler is one of the most popular and, indeed, most perceptive. Often her novels have either a religious or moral theme which runs "slantwise" to the novel itself.

Such is the case with *Saint Maybe*.[19] In this case she tells the story of two brothers. The older brother falls in love and enters a serious relationship. The younger of the two brothers becomes intensely jealous and hints to his senior sibling that his girlfriend is not remaining faithful to him. The older brother, overcome with grief and remorse, having had far too much to drink, drives his car headlong into a wall and is killed. The younger brother goes on to commit much of the next stage of his life to looking after his sister-in-law and her child. Effectively he gives up all other aspirations.

The context is further complicated by the fact that the younger brother has become caught up entirely into an eccentric Christian religious sect. There is no doubting that the influence of this sect, combined with guilt, has encouraged the young man to give up his life in this way—hence the title *Saint Maybe*. The reader's emotions are torn in every direction. The younger brother's behaviour was callous and culpable; the mourning girlfriend is feckless; the religious sect is powerful in its magnetism, but unattractive in its ethos. Undoubtedly the Christian story plays an important part in setting the moral values which drive the younger brother and which help salvage elements of the girlfriend's life, and indeed of her offspring. The story is told with sufficient irony and sophistication, however, as to leave questions in one's mind about the nature of all these moral influences.

Whatever our conclusion may be, it is quite clear that Christian faith can help fashion lives, and in a more positive direction. This is hardly a new discovery and is there within the Christian tradition from patristic times. It is a tradition embraced within Anglicanism by the Caroline moral theologians of the seventeenth century. It was renewed classically in the writings of Kenneth Kirk in the twentieth century. His Bampton Lectures, *The Vision of God* enshrine this tradition most distinctively.[20] At the heart of the argument is the assumption that by fixing our gaze upon the vision of God, as made plain to us through the incarnation in Jesus Christ, then our lives will be "refashioned". They will be refashioned because we ourselves will be "unselfed"; we shall look outward, first of all, to God and that in itself will radically refocus our moral attitudes. In the Caroline tradition, this also led to an integration of theological purpose. Our belief shapes our moral life, and this happens through a clear emphasis on worship, daily prayer, and contemplation. Doctrine, morals, and the liturgy coalesce.

This tradition overlaps, although still retaining its own distinctiveness, with Platonic approaches to morals. So in a parallel manner to Anne Tyler, the novels of Platonist philosopher and novelist Iris Murdoch also often demonstrate how someone whose life has been focused on the *Good* will by instinct be drawn to appropriate moral behaviour.[21] The individual is unselfed. This approach to morals is often known as "eudaimonistic", that is, driven by a focus upon good, goodness, and for the Christian, God. The implications of this for our theme are obvious. It is by the liturgy that the Christian is unselfed. In other words, central to the moral life is the life of prayer and worship; the liturgy stands at the very heart of Christian patterns of discipleship and mission. Prayer, contemplation, and regular attendance at the Eucharist form our moral lives and we proclaim the gospel to others through the way we live, which has been fashioned by our worship.

—

We have set out, then, three "uses of liturgy". Here the word "use" is not intended to be understood in a philosophically utilitarian sense. There is no liturgical calculus, no "greatest liturgy of the greatest number"! Nor indeed is it intended that the liturgy be seen instrumentally. Reverting to our last section, eudaimonistic approaches to morals and doctrine assume that worship and prayer to the God of our Lord Jesus Christ lie at the centre of the purpose for which we are made. Our response to the unmerited grace which we receive is to be drawn into the liturgy through our love for God. Of course, sinfulness means that we are not always so drawn. It also means that the worship and prayer which we offer often fall short of perfection. This returns us to the point from which we began.

Writing of literacy, Richard Hoggart was clear that the significance of literacy was itself a two-edged sword. There will always be good and bad literature, and the influences and effects of poor literature, be it through the media, through pornography, or simply through poor writing—either imaginative or non-fiction—can be dangerous, corrupting, and even catastrophic. Or, to take the argument in a slightly different direction, using the research of Bernstein, if people are exposed to inappropriate or poorly honed linguistic codes, then they will either learn nothing or indeed simply be confused and baffled. Liturgy is open to similar pitfalls. There is a sense in which the language of liturgy is unique and this uniqueness is part of what takes us into the heart of God. Nevertheless, such uniqueness should not be confused with an obtuse or esoteric pattern which makes the liturgy opaque to human response. Similarly, insufficient care in offering and preparing for the liturgy can lead to disastrous results. Austin Farrer, in his Bampton Lectures, argues that Scripture communicates the truths of God, not through propositions, but through key images.[22] Farrer's argument here has an immediate corollary for Christian doctrine and for liturgy and worship. If these images are to speak to us, to form us, and to transform our hearts, then they must be offered in a context where space, care, silence, and prayer are there without limit. Given such richness, worship really will be liturgy, *leitourgia*, that is, *sacrificial service*. The uses of liturgy will be none other than for the service of God.

NOTES

1. First published as "Uses of Liturgy: Worship Nourishing Mission", in *Worship* Vol. 83 No. 3 (May 2009), pp. 234–249, and reproduced here by kind permission of the publisher (<https://www.litpress.org>).

2. Richard Hoggart, *The Uses of Literacy: Aspects of Working-Class Life, with special reference to Publications and Entertainments* (Chatto and Windus, 1957). Some might argue that it is English scholarship rather than sociology, but it probably straddles the boundary.

3. Ibid., p. 337.

4. Ibid., p. 323.

5. Ibid., p. 324.

6. Jeremy Lewis, *Penguin Special: The Life and Times of Allen Lane* (Penguin Books, 2006).

7. Basil Bernstein, *Class, Codes and Control: Theoretical Studies towards a Sociology of Language*, Vol. I (Routledge and Kegan Paul, 1971).

8. Basil Bernstein, "On the Classification and Framing of Educational Knowledge" in Michael F. D. Young (ed.), *Knowledge and Control: New Directions for the Sociology of Education* (Collier-Macmillan, 1971), pp. 47–69.

9. Cf. particularly Grace Davie, *Religion in Modern Europe: A Memory Mutates* (Oxford University Press, 2000), Grace Davie, *Europe: the Exceptional Case: Parameters of Faith in the Modern World* (Darton, Longman and Todd, 2002), and David Martin, *On Secularization: Towards a Revised General Theory* (Ashgate, 2005).

10. Gillian Lindsay, *Flora Thompson: The Story of the Lark Rise Writer* (Robert Hale, 1990), p. 13.

11. Flora Thompson, *Lark Rise to Candleford* (Oxford University Press, 1984), p. 18.

12. Ibid., p. 205.

13. Ibid., p. 207.

14. Ibid., p. 208.

15. Ibid., p. 244.

16. Salley Vickers, *Miss Garnet's Angel* (Harper Collins, 2000).

17. Salley Vickers, *The Other Side of You* (Harper Collins, 2006), p. 182.

18. Ibid.

19. Anne Tyler, *Saint Maybe* (Chatto and Windus, 1991).

20. Kenneth Kirk, *The Vision of God: The Christian Vision of the Summum Bonum* (abridged edition, Longmans Green, 1934).

21. See also both Iris Murdoch, *The Sovereignty of Good* (Routledge and Kegan Paul, 1970), and Iris Murdoch, *Metaphysics as a Guide to Morals* (Chatto and Windus, 1992).

22. Austin Farrer, *The Glass of Vision* (Bampton Lectures 1948, Dacre Press, 1949).

10. NIEBUHR, LITURGY, AND PUBLIC THEOLOGY[1]

Reinhold Niebuhr's name is rarely, if ever, associated with the liturgy. Liturgy is rarely, if ever, associated with public theology: and what do we mean by "public theology" anyway? Is it a new phenomenon generated only in response to modern or even post-modern pluralist societies? Robert Taft, the liturgical theologian, suggests otherwise. He quotes Socrates, the Byzantine historian:

> The Arians . . . held their assemblies outside the city. So each week, whenever there was a feast . . . on which it was customary to hold a synaxis in the churches, they congregated in public squares within the city gates and sang antiphonally odes composed in accord with the Arian belief. And they did this during the greater part of the night . . . John [Chrysostom], concerned lest some of the more simple faithful be drawn away by such odes, set up some of his own people in opposition to them, so that they too, by devoting themselves to nocturnal hymnody, might obscure the effect of the Arians and confirm his own faithful in the profession of their own faith.[2]

Earlier on in the paper in which Robert Taft uses this quotation, he notes:

> We are accustomed to viewing liturgy as something done in church . . . Things were not so in late-Antique Constantinople, when little symbolic or theological impact was assigned to

the Byzantine church building . . . It deals, rather, with what took place *outside the church*, in the processions and services along the principal streets of the capital.[3]

Such stational liturgies were not new, of course, nor were they confined to Constantinople. We know this from the nun Egeria writing of Jerusalem in the fourth century. Indeed, some New Testament critics, following the assumption that the gospels are "passion narratives with an extended introduction", argue that the passion narratives in their present form probably issue from stational liturgies in *first-century* Jerusalem. However we view such theories, it is certainly the case that liturgy was a public event even from the very earliest years of the Christian faith. The Lucan accounts of the earliest Christian community in the Acts of the Apostles confirm this. In Acts 2. 41–2 we read:

> So those who received Peter's word were baptized, and there were added that day about three thousand souls. And they devoted themselves to the apostles' teaching and fellowship, to the breaking of bread and the prayers.

Even allowing for hyperbole and journalese, the public setting and significance of the gospel is clear, issuing here in a new form of liturgical life. Moreover, the setting is deliberately and spectacularly global; earlier in chapter 2 the implied reference back to Babel, with the multitude of languages, places religion in a global setting. A similar social outcome to that recorded here in the Pentecost narrative is assumed in the summary verses which describe the life of the embryonic Christian community (Acts 4. 32 ff.). Peter's preaching is later set within a more deliberate context of public theologizing, which is similarly implicitly liturgical. Indeed, his speeches can be placed alongside Paul's sermon on the Areopagus, reported later (Acts 17. 22). Paul, referring to the altar to an unknown god, sets worship of Christ within and beyond the confines of already existing Greek civic religion, just as Peter before him had addressed his fellow Jews celebrating their own public festival (Deuteronomy 16. 9–12). Jesus' ministry too is undeniably public.

All this stands in clear continuity with Christianity's Jewish roots. It emerges from a longer tradition of prophetic or public religion. Amos, Hosea, and the later prophets were concerned about Israel's reversion to Canaanite public cults and liturgies. Israel's survival required religious purity which directed loyalty to the state. Jesus' encounter with the Pharisees over tribute money stands in this tradition. Indeed, other evidence implies similar public and corporate (that is, not just individualized and pietistic) engagement. Apocalyptic literature (both Daniel and the Revelation to St John, for example) is clearly politically motivated, with the cult never far away. Paul's nuanced advocacy of quietism in Romans 13, Luke's apparent desire to mollify the Roman authorities, the early severe persecutions of the Church—all this and further evidence suggests that the Church through its liturgy and its life directly engaged with politics. At the very least it suggests that the Church was perceived to offer a political challenge.[4] Early Christianity was therefore akin neither to a private world of individuals nor to an exclusive and inner-directed "gnostic" sect. Christianity emerged on the scene in a *public* manner which will have required the beginnings of a theology similarly directed. This makes it clear that "public theology" is intrinsic to Christianity from its inception.

Indeed, many of these examples imply conflict or competition with another public liturgy—be it Arian, Roman, or some form of "Athenian democracy" of the polis, as implied by the setting of the speech on the Areopagus. William Cavanaugh and other contemporary theologians would argue that a comparable rival "liturgy" is there still in the form of a civil religion implied through the operation of the modern nation-state.[5]

The late twentieth century saw a re-emergence of these same issues. It has been classically rehearsed in the works of Martin Marty,[6] to which we shall return. Marty was concerned to clarify the role and nature of "civil religion" in the United States. In debate with Robert Bellah, Marty coined the term "public church" for civil religion. This *public church* engages in *public theology*, which he defined as an attempt "to interpret the life of a people in the light of a transcendent reference".[7] This engagement goes well beyond the realm of self-consciously Christian communities and relates to society more widely. Thus it attempts to order "civil, social, and political life from a theological point of view".[8] Such engagements, one can argue, require a liturgical expression to manifest and support them.

Although Marty's reference point is ostensibly the United States, much of his analysis can be applied more broadly, adjusting it (of course) to the relative degrees in which Christianity is "established" or independent of the state in different cultures and polities. Marty argues that, both in "the academy" and in society more widely, religion has often been defined as a private matter, thus excluding it from many areas of life. This has partly resulted from the use of spatial metaphors which require religion and other "areas" of experience to be differentiated. Instead, Marty uses an analysis developed by Michael Oakeshott when he writes of "modes of experience". So Marty writes, "Oakeshott bids one to think of the world as a continuous, pluralistic conversation, a whole, offering an experience of a world."[9] On this basis Marty establishes the nature and significance of public theology. While this terminology is of recent coinage, it is clear nevertheless that much theological discourse established before Marty's definitions were fully refined falls into the realm of public theology. That is effectively where we began, in fifth-century Byzantium, fourth-century Jerusalem, and the embryonic apostolic and sub-apostolic churches of the New Testament.

Nick Spencer has crystallized what public theology might mean in a recent article in a popular journal:

> The nature of Christian "public witness", and in particular whether it takes place within, without or against the public authorities, depends *not* on what the population thinks—whether people are "Christian" or churchgoing, for example—but rather on whether it embodies values, a concept of the good, that the public recognises and assents to.[10]

In that sense, then, all Christian discourse should be patient of translation into "public theology". This is the point at which Reinhold Niebuhr enters on to the scene. We can begin now to relate two points of the title of this essay; liturgy will have to wait a little longer. On the basis of Marty's definition, Reinhold Niebuhr is classically a public theologian.[11]

—

Interestingly enough, Niebuhr's role as a public theologian emerges most clearly in his work on social ethics, before the publication of his most major theological treatise. In his early works Niebuhr effectively establishes the principles which Marty later expounds. Having been formed in the crucible of Liberal Protestantism, Niebuhr moved gradually away from that tradition, although he reacted too to the neo-orthodoxy of Karl Barth. He did sympathize with Barth's attack on immanentist theologians, since he believed that they undermined the transcendence of God. It was that very transcendence which, for Niebuhr, helped sharpen the "Christian realism" for which he became famous: divine transcendence reminds humanity of its fallibility. Barth's dogmatic theology rooted in revelation, however, ran counter to Niebuhr's emphasis upon the historical, the rational, and the experiential. Niebuhr was very clear about the cultural determinants of human consciousness. For him, Barth's insistence on revelation as the only foundation for theological discourse and his parallel rejection of natural theology were unacceptable. Niebuhr was also critical of the determinism of Marxism, although he was significantly influenced by it as a tool of social and economic analysis. His time as a pastor in Detroit amidst the automobile factories was formative here. So, for example, he writes out of that experience:

> We went through one of the big automobile factories today ... We all want the things which the factory produces and none of us is sensitive enough to care how much in human values the efficiency of the modern factory costs. Beside the brutal facts of modern industrial life, how futile are all our homiletical spoutings. The church is undoubtedly cultivating graces and preserving spiritual amenities in the more protected areas of society. But it isn't changing the essential facts of modern industrial civilisation by a hair's breadth. It isn't even thinking about them.[12]

This precisely captures Marty's definition of public theology which is less concerned with "saving faith" and more concerned with "ordering faith". "Saving faith" might refer to the ways in which an individual is reconciled to God, but is indicative of a theology that does so without reference to our participation in wider social, cultural, or political modes of existence. By contrast, a theological understanding of "ordering faith" helps to offer a critique to society and even to refashion it. Both, of course, are essential, but the above quotation takes us a stage further in Niebuhr's own thought, for it was such insights that helped form his critique of already existing Christian social ethics. Neither the Liberal Protestant tradition nor a pietistic focus upon individual ethics would suffice. Niebuhr was a strong critic of Protestant individualism: "Protestantism's present impotence in qualifying the economic and social life of the nation is due not so much to the pusillanimity of the clerical leaders as to its individualistic traditions."[13] This is where a critical use of Marxism, with its analysis of social forces, was one of Niebuhr's essential tools. His critique of individualism emerges most sharply in Niebuhr's *Moral Man and Immoral Society* (1932). In this book Niebuhr is determined to press home the need for a Christian social ethic. He is clear that a focus uniquely upon the individual cannot achieve this.

It may be that Niebuhr makes the modern assumption identified by both Marty and Cavanaugh: the religious and secular are seen as two entirely separate spheres.[14] The state is concerned with what is properly "public" whereas religion is relegated to being a matter of individual conscience within the private realm. The Church is thus privatized and is no longer seen as having a distinctly public function. Hidden, then, is the sense of rivalry between different public liturgies which we have encountered in the New Testament and in the sub-apostolic period—the Church now has no public role and the state disavows possessing a rival, albeit secularized, "liturgical" function. Niebuhr is intent on bridging what he presumes to be a divide between a privatized Church and public life, but he does not do this by asserting the claim to truth of the Church, instead seeking to develop a Christian social ethic that will be intelligible within and to a democratic state.[15] Following from this is the related distinction in Niebuhr's mind between Catholic sacramental theology, which touches on the magical, and a more rational Christian *realist* vision, which saw the Church, with its account of human sinfulness, as being necessary to moderate the pride of public institutions.

Niebuhr thus moves the Church away from a concern with the merely private and individual and reasserts its prophetic and social role. Niebuhr does not deny the significance of the individual, and indeed elsewhere devotes space to it,[16] but he argues that any morality that is purely individual is impotent. This means that a Christian's engagement with politics is unavoidable. He states this with some irony: "The real problem for the Christian is not how anyone as good as he can participate in unethical political activity but how anyone as sinful as he can dare to set himself as a judge of his fellow man."[17] A similar insight led to one of Niebuhr's most famous aphorisms, on this occasion about democracy: "Man's capacity for justice makes democracy possible; but man's inclination to injustice makes democracy necessary."[18] Niebuhr is keen to sharpen the distinctive issues that need to be taken into account in developing an effective social ethic. Issues of individual ethics often contrast with those undergirding a social ethic. So, at root, Niebuhr argues that the individual will almost invariably behave more morally than will society. A social ethic is necessary because individualistic ethical motivation alone is insufficient. For society is not an aggregate of individuals but a body. Bodies, as wholes, behave differently from the separate individuals from which they are constituted.

This social ethic is essentially lived out in such a manner as to undermine institutional injustice. Niebuhr thus writes of national egotism and of the impossibility of nations being able to aspire to social knowledge and conscience. He notes that even social peace is little more than a *pax Romana*, hiding its will-to-power under the veil of its will-to-peace. The "will-to-live becomes the will-to-power" and ultimately the "will-to-power of competing national groups is the cause of the international anarchy which the moral sense of mankind has thus far vainly striven to overcome."[19] The key to Niebuhr's social ethical thought is the dialectic of love and justice. Justice embodies but never completely fulfils the requirements of love. Love widens the idea and application of justice, but it cannot be substituted for the institution of justice. It is the perfect love seen in Christ which grounds this. Niebuhr is summed up by William Werpehowski thus:

> How can anyone deny that Niebuhr's is the quintessential example of a political ethic of free responsibility? His vision, one might say, never rests in uncritical contentment. Justice may be realized in human societies with no positive limit to it set in advance. Yet all achievements fall short and are

judged by the law of love, since they are all tainted by sin
. . . and so forth.[20]

This makes abundantly clear the reasons for seeing Niebuhr as a classic example of a "public theologian". Niebuhr is clear that theology must be dialectic in its response to the world and to the nature of our humanity. Without a clear anthropological and cultural analysis it is impossible to relate God to the created order and to human society. For these reasons Niebuhr did not see himself primarily as a theologian, but first and foremost as a Christian social thinker.

—

Undoubtedly Niebuhr's anthropological starting point did not lead him to engage at depth with ecclesiological issues. This means that there are few sustained reflections on the significance of liturgy and worship in his work. There are certainly frequent references to preaching; Niebuhr was himself a powerful orator both in the pulpit and in the lecture theatre. Niebuhr and liturgy, however, are rarely placed alongside each other. Nonetheless, recent developments in liturgical theology suggest that Niebuhr's theological and ethical analysis of humanity ought to be brought into conjunction with the liturgical tradition. Increasingly, the formative and transformative nature of the liturgy is being stressed.[21] The Eucharist re-presents the central mystery of the Christian faith—the passion, death, and resurrection of Jesus Christ. In this re-presentation people are taken into the mystery and this forms both their being and their living. Niebuhr's writing does not approach theology from this direction, and his reflections upon liturgy often tend to reflect the Liberal Protestant world in which he was nurtured. He was thus weak on ecclesiology and therefore also on the doxological roots of theology. At this point, then, we shall respond to some of the critical reflections of his most recent theological detractors. We may then analyse some of his own references to the liturgy before seeing how his ethical and theological analysis might be brought into a clearer liturgical conjunction as an integral part of a public theology. As we have seen, this conjunction was part of the Christian tradition from its earliest days.

One of Niebuhr's sharpest recent critics is Stanley Hauerwas. Hauerwas is clear that the key role of the Church is "to be the Church". It is to witness to the gospel of Jesus Christ and so Christology itself stands at the centre. The Christian is not there to engage with the state; that, Hauerwas believes, is one of the key flaws in Niebuhr's work. The gospel, and Christology in particular, are compromised by the political, cultural, and anthropological world with which Niebuhr engages. Hauerwas roots his analysis in a strong ecclesiology which is partly dependent upon the work of John Howard Yoder. Yoder is clear that the Christian Church cannot disavow all political responsibility. Some engagement with the state and thus with politics remains essential, but Yoder's resistance remains passive. Almost certainly, Niebuhr would have seen Yoder's non-violent, passive resistance as colluding with such coercion. Here we can see the tension between the two approaches most vividly. Yoder may be reprimanded for colluding with coercion, Niebuhr for not taking the Church sufficiently seriously as a body bearing witness of itself and challenging the values of the state.

There is a sharp point of contention here. Both Yoder and Hauerwas are keen to develop a proper ecclesiological basis for their theological ethics. This requires the Church to set itself apart and model a life of holiness which takes its point of departure from Christology. Such setting itself apart and embracing non-violence begins with the Christian Church living key elements including forgiveness and reconciliation. Only by learning how to live through such practices can we as a people come to see the violence often present in our lives that would otherwise go unnoticed.[22] There is, then, a proper self-consciousness with which the Church needs to engage.

The criticism is thus that Niebuhr failed to take these elements of the Church's witness seriously enough. How, therefore, can the Church respond effectively as a witnessing community and not simply as a pressure group aimed at resisting or attacking political policies head on? By taking the state as a given and then offering a critique, the Church may appear to accept the basis of society as a democracy (in the case of the United States) and attempt simply to amend its modus operandi through political means. Hauerwas sees this as compromising the challenge of the gospel. The gospel is embodied in a people—the Church—who exemplify a more excellent form of social existence. In an interesting analysis, William Werpehowski offers a critical approach which seeks out the strengths and weaknesses of both theological enterprises. So he argues that Niebuhr arrives at his position "because he tends not to place the resurrection of Jesus Christ in history, even though historical Christian faith presupposes it". Later Werpehowski notes:

> My analysis suggests that without considered attention to concrete practices in a church that witnesses to a new life promised and present in the risen Christ, and without an integrally related attention to what God is doing in the world in calling political agencies to repentance and transformation beyond their narrower faiths, political freedom is bereft.[23]

Although Werpehowski does not spell it out, the performance of the liturgy must be at the heart of this, but so must an engagement with the relativities of the world. Indeed, this returns us to the very beginning of our reflections where we saw how in apostolic, sub-apostolic, and patristic times the liturgy stood central to what we might now call a "public theology". Liturgy, worship, and prayer mark off the Christian Church from other human agencies and so are crucial to any public living and proclaiming of the gospel. This has been ignored by many liturgical theologians as well as systematicians. Bernd Wannenwetsch offers an interesting analysis of this linkage of liturgy and public life which mirrors something of the critique of Hauerwas and Yoder alongside that of Niebuhr noted earlier. He sees three models for the relationship between worship and politics: first, religion is *counter-cultural*—the Augustinian tradition is the clear example here; second, as an *ideal type* religion sets out a pattern for the ordering of society—here William Temple is cited; finally, the Church *paradigmatically* lives the gospel, witnessing to the redemptive pattern which God establishes in Jesus—this model includes Hauerwas and Yoder. Within this analysis, Niebuhr would fit most obviously within the Augustinian tradition, following that tradition through its Lutheran trajectory. Wannenwetsch argues for a different approach where "liturgical experience spills over in a complex and manifold way".[24] This would allow for a development of the Augustinian tradition which does not too easily baptize the values of democratic society, but which develops Niebuhr's social ethical critique and allows it to be deployed more effectively through the liturgy as public theology. In other words, it does not simply afford the public realm an autonomy distinct from all theology.

This sort of pattern has been commended by Edward Foley, who specifically mentions Niebuhr in this context. Foley's argument is that worship can itself be public theology if it is grounded in the public ministry of Jesus, it is at least a public event, and it is enacted for the sake of the world. Foley argues that churches are engaged in a ritual form of worship whether they like it or not, and therefore that requires of them some care in what they rehearse theologically in that worship. So we must be clear about what we are intending to articulate in the liturgy. It must be anchored in the tradition; it must be congruent with the rest of a community's public life; it must be engaged in a mutually critical public dialogue. This final point stands four-square within the Niebuhrian tradition. Foley notes that Niebuhr largely saw apologetics and social ethics as sufficient, but also sees a seed for further development in Niebuhr's own work, and notably in his Gifford Lectures, which set out his theological anthropology most fully.[25] Foley refers specifically to Niebuhr's "distinctions between the vitalistic and the rational as a way to underscore the importance of symbolic mediation for the good not just of a church but of a republic".[26] We shall return to this later.

At certain points Niebuhr does refer to the liturgy; however, the majority of references by Niebuhr to worship focus upon preaching. There are extant recordings of Niebuhr lecturing and preaching, and the effect is electrifying. Richard Fox, Niebuhr's biographer, captures this emphasis sharply when he writes:

> His own ecclesiology, sketchy as it was, remained fundamentally Protestant in its stress on symbolism. There was no real presence of God in the sacrament, but a symbolic representation of God's presence. The church was a community of grace, but grace was mediated more through the word that was preached than through the eucharist that was broken and shared. Niebuhr's grace was verbal, active—a grace that confronted the believer and challenged even

the Church itself. A sacramental Church was too liable to passivity, self-satisfaction, too prone to believe itself sanctified. Beginning with his Detroit pastorate Niebuhr therefore stressed the Jewish prophetic "roots of Christianity".[27]

This is very clear from entries in his stylized diary of those early years. He writes of his attendance at a funeral in a Roman Catholic church in a manner which is both critical of his own tradition and of the Mass:

> I don't think the mass is so satisfying as a well conducted Protestant funeral service . . . But it is certainly immeasurably superior to the average Protestant service with its banalities and sentimentalities. Religion is poetry . . . [however,] one must not forget that the truth is not only vivified but also corrupted by the poetic symbol for it is only one step from a vivid symbol to the touch of magic. The priest does, after all, deal with magic.[28]

Here, Niebuhr's analysis is unsophisticated. The use of the term "magic" is unfortunate. He rejects what he calls magic for a more subtle appreciation of God's presence in the "workaday world". He is faltering after a deeper sense of the sacramental than his own tradition often offers, but he is wary and even suspicious of Catholic sacramentalism as he understands it. As an Anglophile (married to an English woman), he knew Anglicanism well and was appreciative of a patterned and more formal liturgical usage: "The idea that a formless service is more spontaneous and therefore more religious than a formal one is disproved in my own experience."[29] Nevertheless, here (as elsewhere) he does not develop this by exploring the significance of a formal liturgy or of the sacramental tradition. Later, indeed, he reveals his own Protestantism in his response to the controversy over the Church of England's "deposited" (and so non-authorized) Prayer Book of 1927:

> Here is the Episcopal Church which many of us have counted blessed because it was the one bridge over the chasm which separates Catholicism and Protestantism. But the chasm is now revealed as too wide for any bridge. Cooperation with the

Catholic demands connivance with religious practices which reduce religion to magic. No wonder the Protestant laymen in Parliament threw the revised prayer book out. How can anyone in the year of our Lord 1927 be seriously exercised over the problem of the "real presence" in the Eucharist?[30]

This encapsulates Niebuhr's rather naïve understanding of sacramentality. Elsewhere, however, he reflects upon this and makes a tentative link between the moral life and worship:

Religion is a reaction to life's mysteries and a reverence before the infinitudes of the universe. Without ethical experience the infinite is never defined in ethical terms, but the soul which is reverent and morally vital at the same time learns how to apprehend the infinite in terms of holiness and worship a God who transcends both our knowledge and our conscience.[31]

Here is a much clearer hint towards a sacramental embracing of the principles of his ethical theory and the need to express these through the liturgy. There is a mystifying dysfunction between these various reflections. There appears to be a proper seeking after a sacramental sense; Niebuhr is engaged by the poetic, and his own writing, preaching, and prayer indicate a real sensitivity not only to the power of words, but to a deeper sense of glimpsing God in the material things of everyday experience. His Protestant formation, however, frightens him away from what he feels inevitably will direct the Church towards a "magical" understanding of liturgy, worship, and theology. Perhaps by exploring this tension we can develop a clearer sense of how Niebuhr's social ethical critique may be used more directly in liturgy as public theology.

—

Edward Foley points to Niebuhr's exploration of the polarities of vitalism and rationalism. By vitalism Niebuhr appears to mean the basic natural life force in humanity, which can then be constrained by rational thought.

This is present most explicitly in his Gifford Lectures, but it appears elsewhere in his specifically ethical writings, where Niebuhr balances the influence of romanticism and utilitarian rationalism in producing his own framework of "prophetic religion".[32] This is where Niebuhr is directly critical of the Liberal Protestant tradition in which he was nurtured. This tradition abandoned the proper theological elements of the mythical symbolism at the heart of the gospel which helped interpret the nature of our humanity with all its aspirations and fallibilities. It attempted to remove these elements, separating history and theology and transposing Jesus so that he became instead the good man who walked the shores of the Sea of Galilee; he simply exemplified human goodness. But by so limiting both Jesus and the Christian religion, the transcendent is excluded. Alongside this, the power of evil, the will-to-power, and the coercive elements within human society are played down or ignored, thus producing an inappropriate "ideal" which ignores human fallibility and so subverts that fallibility which is central to Niebuhr's Christian realism.

In his Gifford Lectures, exploring the two polarities of vitalism and rationalism, Niebuhr notes the vitality present in all creatures but identifies the specific nature of human vitalism through focusing on our self-transcendence. It is the way that this vitalism works within us that defines human creativity. God is the source of this vitality, as well as of order and rationality. Niebuhr reviews a number of developments within modernity, including the protest of the Romantics against rationalism,[33] and both the contribution and deficiencies of Marxism. He is clear that it is impossible to resolve fully the tension between vitality and form, between vitalism and rationalism.[34] Even so, it is from this tension that his social theory grows, embracing the cultural and anthropological but allowing for the vitality which is God-given to free us from a sterile rationalism. From this emerges a symbolic mediation which embraces the patterns set out in orthodox Christian thought; the work of Christ is not exhausted in a Liberal Protestant picture of Jesus as "the good man", nor indeed in attempts to root all in rediscovering the historical Jesus. The pattern of salvation in Christ transcends a purely rationalistic framework.

Ironically, it appears that in his own living out of the Christian gospel Niebuhr was unable to engage with how this understanding might have an immediate relationship with liturgy and worship. The roots of this may lie in his own declared rejection of the term "theologian" for his work. As he energetically embraced the world, he was steered away from any self-conscious reflection upon the nature of the Church. For many this remains the most refreshing and distinguishing feature of Niebuhr's undoubted theological contribution, despite his own protestations. As a theologian he almost certainly influenced politics on both sides of the Atlantic more than any other twentieth-century Christian writer. Ironically, however, this seems to have constrained him liturgically. The liturgy remained, for him, largely an exercise for the church community except inasmuch as it was the platform for prophetic preaching.

Liturgy is, however, not a purely ecclesial community event. It is a public event and at certain moments Niebuhr recognized this, as we have seen. What he did not respond to was the performative nature of the liturgy, and thus its place within a developed public theology. The performative element of the liturgy means its capacity to be formative and transformative of the wider community. This comes as a result of the liturgical event itself and through the potentially transformative power of the community of faith, constituted by that event.

There may be ways in which public liturgies—occasional offices, processions, memorials, inductions of new ministers, "ways of the cross"—can be made to impinge on society at different levels. The main argument, however, lies deeper. The liturgy is the means by which the Church receives itself from beyond. It creates a medium which can literally embody Niebuhr's critical insights and so can also be transformative in its public interactions. Liturgy within a clear ecclesiological framework can make his critique still more potent. Niebuhr's refreshing ability to look outward from the Church, challenging society, meant that his ecclesiology was virtually non-existent. We see this in the naïve way in which he understands sacramentality as a form of "magic" and yet, at the same time, hints at some form of sacramentality by rooting the gospel in the things of everyday life. In this sense he was not a theologian, at least not an ecclesial theologian, as he himself declared. He was, however, undoubtedly a public theologian—assuming, that is, that public theology can be strengthened through a further key liturgical insight. The Eucharist is the key performative Christian liturgy and is unitive not only in bringing together humanity and God, but also in bringing humanity itself together in solidarity. In doing this, the Eucharist also transgresses international boundaries and subverts the national will-to-power and rivalry, or subsequent rivalry, which Niebuhr so clearly identified. By embracing this theological insight, Niebuhr's theology can be effectively enriched, strengthening the Church and giving a clearer sense of ecclesiology.[35]

As Foley argues, the liturgy itself is, or ought to be, a crucial element within any public theology. The message is clear for the Church. What message do we broadcast through our liturgy? Does it measure up to those images with which we began, in fourth-century Byzantium, at the Areopagus, or indeed in Jesus' own ministry? Hauerwas' and Yoder's critique of Reinhold Niebuhr may miss the mark overall. Nevertheless, that critique may hit its target in encouraging a more adequate ecclesiology, rooted in a performative liturgy, which will focus Niebuhr's theological anthropology, and not only through the preached word but actually within corporate worship itself. The Eucharist re-presents the central mystery of the Christian faith—the passion, death, and resurrection of Jesus Christ. It was the impact of that mystery that ultimately shaped Niebuhr's social ethics. How can the liturgy reflect Niebuhr's critique performatively? That is, how can the Church as a community formed by its worship live out in its daily life that performative challenge?

NOTES

1. First published as "Niebuhr, Liturgy, and Public Theology" in Stephen Platten and Richard Harries (eds.), *Reinhold Niebuhr and Contemporary Politics: God and Power* (OUP, 2010), pp. 102–116, ISBN: 9780199571833; reproduced here by kind permission of Oxford University Press (<https://global.oup.com>).

2. The Byzantine historian Socrates, quoted by Robert Taft SJ in *Liturgy in Old Constantinople: Glimpses of a Lost World* (Alcuin Club, 2008), p. 4.

3. Ibid., p. 3 (emphasis original).

4. See, e.g., the essays in Richard A. Horsley's edited volumes: *Paul and Politics: Ekklesia, Israel, Imperium, Interpretation* (Continuum, 2000), and *Paul and Empire: Religion and Power in Roman Imperial Society* (Continuum, 1997).

See also Wayne A. Meeks, *The First Urban Christians: The Social World of the Apostle Paul* (Yale University Press, 1984).

5. William T. Cavanaugh, *Theopolitical Imagination: Discovering the Liturgy as a Political Act in an Age of Global Consumerism* (T&T Clark, 2002), p. 31. See also Cavanaugh, "Killing for the Telephone Company: Why the Nation-State is Not the Keeper of the Common Good", in *Modern Theology* Vol. 20 No. 2 (April 2004), pp. 243–274.

6. Cf. Martin E. Marty, *The Public Church: Mainline-Evangelical-Catholic* (Crossroad Press, 1981).

7. Ibid., p. 16.

8. Ibid.

9. Martin E. Marty, "Religion: A Private Affair, in Public Affairs", public lecture to the Center for the Study of Religion and American Culture, October 1992, published in *Religion and American Culture* 3 (Summer 1993), pp. 115–127, and online (<http://www.illuminos.com/mem/selectPapers/religionPublicPrivate.html>).

10. Nick Spencer, "A Private Affair?", in *Third Way* Vol. 31 No. 5 (June 2008), p. 29, and online (<https://thirdway.hymnsam.co.uk/editions/june-2008/features/a-private-affair.aspx>).

11. See Daniel M. Bell Jnr., "State and Civil Society", in Peter Scott and William T. Cavanaugh (eds.), *The Blackwell Companion to Political Theology* (Blackwell, 2004), p. 432. Bell sees Niebuhr as the classic exemplification of public theology in the twentieth century.

12. Reinhold Niebuhr, *Leaves from the Notebook of a Tamed Cynic* (Harper and Row, 1929), pp. 78–79.

13. Ibid., p. 96.

14. Cavanaugh, *Theopolitical Imagination*, p. 31.

15. William T. Cavanaugh, "Church", in *Blackwell Companion*, pp. 400–401.

16. Reinhold Niebuhr, *The Nature and Destiny of Man: A Christian Interpretation*, Vol. I (Nisbet, 1941), III pp. 57–8. The two volumes of *The Nature and Destiny of Man* are based on Niebuhr's Gifford Lectures (Edinburgh, 1938–1940).

17. Reinhold Niebuhr, in *Christianity and Society* (Spring 1938).

18. Reinhold Niebuhr, *The Children of Light and the Children of Darkness* (Nisbet, 1945), p. ix.

19. Reinhold Niebuhr, *Moral Man and Immoral Society* (Scribners, 1932), pp. 18–19.

20. William Werpehowski, "Reinhold Niebuhr" in *Blackwell Companion*, p. 188.

21. Cf. A Report of the Church of England's Liturgical Commission, *Transforming Worship: Living the New Creation* (GS1651, 2007). Available online (<https://churchofengland.org/media/1251048/gs1651.pdf>).

22. Stanley Hauerwas, *Dispatches from the Front* (Duke University Press, 1994), p. 130.

23. Werpehowski, "Reinhold Niebuhr", p. 192.

24. Bernd Wannenwetsch, "Liturgy" in *Blackwell Companion*, pp. 87–88.

25. Edward Foley, Capuchin, "Engaging the Liturgy of the World: Worship as Public Theology", in *Studia Liturgica* Vol. 38 No. 1 (2008), p. 35.

26. Ibid., pp. 47–48.

27. Richard Fox, "Reinhold Niebuhr: The Living of Christian Realism", in Richard Harries (ed.), *Reinhold Niebuhr and the Issues of Our Time* (Mowbray, 1986), pp. 20–21.

28. Niebuhr, *Leaves*, pp. 32–33.

29. Ibid., p. 61.

30. Ibid., p. 156.

31. Ibid., p. 55.

32. See, for example, Reinhold Niebuhr, *An Interpretation of Christian Ethics* (SCM Press, 1936), pp. 213ff.

33. For a reference to this in a specifically Christian context, see Stephen Platten, "One Intellectual Breeze: Coleridge and a new Apologetic", in *Theology* Vol. 111 Issue 863 (September/October 2008), pp. 323–335.

34. Cf. Niebuhr, *The Nature and Destiny of Man*, Vol. I, especially pp. 27–56.

35. Cavanaugh, *Theopolitical Imagination*, pp. 49–50.

AFTERWORD

Most academic studies of liturgy, including many of my own writings, examine the details of the history of Christian worship; even those that address what is called liturgical theology are often quite narrow in their focus and sometimes make little connection with ordinary people's actual experience of public worship.

What is refreshing about the collection of essays by Stephen Platten that we have just read is their sheer breadth. They certainly draw on various aspects of liturgical history and theology, but this is set within a very much wider context than one might have expected. It is not just that they touch on broader theological issues and aspects of church life, but they also range far and wide in making connections to other fields of study and other areas of human experience. Who would have expected to find in a book concerned with liturgical issues Austin Farrer and Reinhold Niebuhr rubbing shoulders with Gerald Durrell and Evelyn Waugh, to name but a few of the authors appearing in these pages? The essays are also infused throughout with the knowledge and wisdom gained from Stephen's many years of practical liturgical experience as both priest and bishop.

Paul F. Bradshaw
Emeritus Professor of Liturgy
University of Notre Dame

GENERAL INDEX

INDEX OF BIBLE REFERENCES